RECOGNISE WHAT?

RECOGNISE WHAT?

Arguments to acknowledge Aborigines, but not recognise Aboriginal culture or rights, in the Australian Constitution

Edited by Gary Johns

Connor Court Publishing

PO Box 224W
Ballarat VIC 3350
sales@connorcourt.com
www.connorcourt.com

ISBN: 9781925138238 (pbk.)

Cover design by Ian James

Printed in Australia

CONTENTS

Acknowledgements

This book, *Recognise What?* commenced life as a paper, *History yes, Culture no*, presented by the editor to the 2013 Samuel Griffith Society conference held in Sydney. The Samuel Griffith Society is a venerable group, distinguished in law and politics, which provides a conservative and federalist forum for debate about the Australian Constitution. The Society does not, however, formulate policy.

The question of the recognition of Aborigines in the Australian Constitution seemed a fitting place at which to present the paper. I am grateful to The Honourable Ian Callinan AC QC, president of the Society, for his invitation and the valuable discussion that ensued.

I am indebted to each of the authors for their enthusiastic agreement to present their ideas and arguments under the general auspice of what I call the limited Yes case: to acknowledge Aborigines prior occupation in a preamble to, but not recognise Aboriginal culture or rights in, the Australian Constitution. There is no caucus, however, each author presents their preferred position.

The arguments, presented in clear and direct prose, deserve a wide audience. They should stimulate debate throughout the land, which is as it should be when a government embarks on a referendum that requires a vote of all Australian citizens.

Sadly, Bryan Pape passed away during the preparation of this book. The book is dedicated to his good work in constitutional law and politics.

Gary Johns
Brisbane
May 2014

Recognise What? Inc

Readers can follow the debate and participate as it unfolds by logging on to our website and blog at

Recognisewhat.org.au

Foreword

It would be as presumptuous for me to suggest that I had any expertise in Italian or German or Chinese culture as it would be for me to make any similar claim in respect of Australian indigenous culture. Notwithstanding my lack of expertise in the first three, I very much enjoy the master works of Italian painting, the music of Bach and the delicacy of Chinese porcelain and ink scrolls. In the same way, many Asian people understand, listen to and play Western music. When did you last see and hear a symphony orchestra playing Western music in which some of the players, often quite a large number of the players, were not obviously ethnically East Asian? Why is it that the English language is so broadly used and its use increasing across the world? Why is all of this so? The answer, in my view, is not simply an accident or accidents of history. It is in some circles now, unfashionable to suggest that these cultural triumphs have occurred because of intrinsic cultural merit or utility. One thing is however certain, that none of these consequences is a consequence of imposition. A toleration and appreciation of the customs, laws, languages, practices and arts of others is and can never be compellable.

The questions that I have posed are all of course highly relevant to the various proposals for the introduction into the Australian Constitution of provisions to recognise the Aboriginal people and their way of life, beliefs and practices in the Australian Constitution.

In this collection of scholarly and thoughtful essays, marshalled by Dr Gary Johns, including one by himself, the case, a very strong case I think, is made against any such constitutional recognition.

Any non-indigenous person living in Australia today, who did not have concern for the general plight of indigenous people in this country, would be heartless. But the lot of indigenous people will not be improved by constitutional recognition. I doubt whether there would be any person alive today who did not know that the settlement of Australia by Aboriginal and Torres Strait Islander peoples long preceded occupation by others. Nor is there anything unique in any way about a relationship of any people who live on land, at any place at any time, between them and the land. To suggest that cultures, languages and heritages need to earn respect because of their intrinsic virtues or attractions is to risk a charge of academic or political heresy. All of the authors in this publication are prepared to run, and do I think surmount, that risk.

Additionally, the essays in the collection provide information in some instances – I will not say suppressed – but overlooked or deliberately disregarded by some proponents of the proposals.

It would be repetitive for me to rehearse what is better said by the authors, but some of the issues discussed are of particular interest to me. Professor James Allan warns against any constitutional amendment for the reason that any of the proposed amendments would inevitably empower unelected judges in an undemocratic way. He is right in saying that the discovery by the High Court after some 90 or so years, of a constitutional freedom of speech, buried deep in the text and structure of the Constitution was, to say the least, extraordinary. If such an implied freedom can be found to be nesting in the text and the structure of the Constitution by all-seeing and all-wise moderne judges, anything is possible in the constitutional jurisprudence of future successive High Courts.

If there is one predisposition that any democratic lawyer should have, it is towards equal treatment of those who come before the judges. That is not to say that a judge should not impose penalties under the criminal law which take account of the disadvantaged circumstances of a particular convicted person. I do not know of any sentencing legislation in this country, except for some enactments which prescribe mandatory penalties, that do not provide for that. Even so, none of those mandatory penalties depend in any way upon the ethnicity of the convicted person. Any constitutional provision which might in any way be sought to justify a different law for peoples of different ethnicity on grounds of that ethnicity, should be resisted. This must be so for reasons of fairness and social cohesion, as well as clarity of application.

One suggestion for change is that recognition be by way of a preamble only. A practical and important legal objection to this is well made by the late and lamented Bryan Pape in his contribution to this publication. I have another reservation about it which is not dispelled by a defence that it would be merely symbolic. Mere symbols can be a distraction. They may give those who raise and participants in them, a warm middle-class glow of virtue, but in reality they are shadows, not matters of substance. Nonetheless they can be distractions, absorbing for their erection, energy, effort and political will otherwise and better directed towards the genuine improvement, and full participation of indigenous people in Australian society.

I Callinan AC
Brisbane
May 2014

Introduction

In 2014 or soon thereafter, Australians will be asked by the Australian Government to consider a proposition to recognise Aborigines and Torres Strait Islanders (hereinafter, Aborigines) in the Australian Constitution. *Recognise* is the officially sanctioned and government-funded campaign for Aboriginal recognition in the Australian Constitution. It pursues a 'Yes' case tantamount to a bill of rights for one group based on race. It is potentially very harmful to the nation and to Aborigines.

Recognise seeks to promote not only recognition of prior occupation, but of characteristics of Aborigines such that would create separate and special rights for Aborigines. It does so on the basis that Aborigines are assumed to have a unique culture. That may be so, but the historical record reveals that while the Aboriginal culture may include admirable aspects, it also includes a number of less than attractive beliefs and practices. The record reveals, for example, that a major part of Aboriginal culture rests on 'demand sharing' or 'humbugging', which means that, whatever one earns others have a right to. A rich man gains cousins that he may not have seen for ages, these bludge off him, leaving him as poor as when he started. Young men and women bully their grandparents for pension money. If humbugging is the measure of culture in the *Recognise* proposition, there is little of it that should be encouraged, let alone be preserved in law.

This book seeks to explain risks associated with the proposal endorsed by *Recognise* and others, and to promote an alternative. A measured and feasible response to a desire among some Aborigines for recognition is to acknowledge, in a preamble to the Constitution, the historical fact that Aborigines occupied the continent, now known as Australia, prior to its occupation by the British and later, peoples of the world. The apparently modest proposal has its detractors, who fear that it too, much like bolder proposals, may damage the Australian political fabric. Nevertheless, it is a modest attempt to assuage the desires among a section of the electorate to do something for Aborigines.

Recognise What? informs readers of aspects of Aboriginal culture that are best left in the past. At the same time, it challenges the reader to understand that recognising Aboriginal culture would support behaviour unacceptable to, indeed unlawful for, other Australians. Recognition may allow punishments for criminal acts to be lessened for Aborigines, or unfairly allow an Aborigine access to their child following divorce between an Aborigine and a non-Aborigine. Presently, differences in people's culture are taken into account in Australian courts. Constitutional recognition may limit courts freedom to judge the difference. It would provide an incentive to play the race card.

Ambit claims

The Gillard Government selected an 'Expert Panel' to advise on changes to the Constitution to recognise Aborigines. The report, *Recognising Aboriginal and Torres Strait Islander Peoples in the Constitution* (January 2012), recommended that Australians should vote in a referendum as follows:

> 1. Repeal Section 25. At present the section reads: 'Provisions as to races disqualified from voting: ... if by the law of any State all persons of any race are

disqualified from voting at elections for the more numerous House of the Parliament of the State, then, in reckoning the number of the people of the State or of the Commonwealth, persons of that race resident in that State shall not be counted'.

2. Repeal Section 51(xxvi). At present the section reads: '... the people of any race for whom it is deemed necessary to make special laws'.

3. That a new section 51A be inserted, along the following lines: 'Section 51A Recognition of Aboriginal and Torres Strait Islander peoples:

- Recognising that the continent and its islands now known as Australia were first occupied by Aboriginal and Torres Strait Islander peoples.

- Acknowledging the continuing relationship of Aboriginal and Torres Strait Islander peoples with their traditional lands and waters.

- Respecting the continuing cultures, languages and heritage of Aboriginal and Torres Strait Islander peoples.

- Acknowledging the need to secure the advancement of Aboriginal and Torres Strait Islander peoples.

- The Parliament shall, subject to this Constitution, have power to make laws for the peace, order and good government of the Commonwealth with respect to Aboriginal and Torres Strait Islander peoples.'

4. That a new section 116A be inserted, along the following lines: 'Section 116A Prohibition of racial discrimination:

- The Commonwealth, a State or a Territory shall not discriminate on the grounds of race, colour or ethnic or national origin.

Subsection (1) does not preclude the making of laws or measures for the purpose of overcoming disadvantage, ameliorating the effects of past discrimination, or protecting the cultures, languages or heritage of any group.'

5. That a new section 127A be inserted, along the following lines: 'Section 127A Recognition of languages:

- The national language of the Commonwealth of Australia is English.

- The Aboriginal and Torres Strait Islander languages are the original Australian languages, a part of our national heritage.'

Timetable

The Panel's agenda was very bold indeed and even its sponsor, the Gillard Government, came to realise that the panel was not so much expert as radical. Realising that there was insufficient public support for constitutional recognition as proposed by the panel, indeed, possibly for any proposal, it postponed the referendum question. Instead, the Gillard Government sponsored the *Aboriginal and Torres Strait Islander Peoples Recognition Act 2013* which stated, 'further engagement with Aboriginal and Torres Strait Islander peoples and other Australians is required to refine proposals for a referendum and to build the support necessary for successful constitutional change'.

The 'expert' version of recognition was watered down in the Act to read:

(1) The Parliament, on behalf of the people of Australia, recognises that the continent and the islands now known as Australia were first occupied by Aboriginal and Torres Strait Islander peoples.

(2) The Parliament, on behalf of the people of Australia, acknowledges the continuing relationship of Aboriginal and Torres Strait Islander peoples with their traditional lands and waters.

(3) The Parliament, on behalf of the people of Australia, acknowledges and respects the continuing cultures, languages and heritage of Aboriginal and Torres Strait Islander peoples.

While the 'menu' of recognition is less extensive than that recommended by the Expert Panel, it remains problematic. The form of recognition in part (1) is, arguably, the greatest degree of recognition that could be achieved without affecting the rights of other Australians. Even so, such recognition should be confined to a preamble, the stated intention of which would be that it not be used to interpret the Constitution. The Act also canvasses, in parts (2) and (3), Aboriginal characteristics, the recognition of which would cause significant problems. Further, there is no clarity provided in the Act as to whether any words would be confined to a Preamble or be placed in the Constitution.

Tony Abbott, then Opposition leader, in his second reading speech to the Act, admitted that it would 'be a challenge to find a form of recognition which satisfies reasonable people as being fair to all. It won't necessarily be straightforward to acknowledge the first Australians without creating new categories of discrimination which we must avoid, because no Australian should feel like a stranger in their own country.' It is indeed a challenge for, now Prime Minister, Abbott to arrive at an acceptable form of words.

The Act also established a process to review readiness for support for a referendum. A Joint Select Committee of the Parliament chaired by Ken Wyatt (Hasluck, WA, Liberal Party) is undertaking consultation. At the same time, former deputy Prime Minister John Anderson is leading a panel to conduct a review of public support.

The review panel is to work with the Joint Select Committee on constitutional recognition. The review panel is required to provide a report to the Minister for Indigenous Affairs, Senator Scullion by 28 September 2014. The government will announce a draft amendment to the Constitution for public consultation sometime thereafter.

Responses

Various chapters in this book refer to the Expert Panel's recommendations or the Recognition Act because, at the time of publication, these are the only proposals in the public arena. The responses to the various proposals, organised in four sections, contain essays each of 2,000 words.

The first section, **Questioning Aboriginal culture**, contains two essays. Ron Brunton undercuts the recognition rationale that rests on *cultural continuity*, a great deal of which, he argues, is a myth. Alistair Crooks reflects on earlier Aboriginal culture and argues that any attempt at its recognition would constitute an *Aboriginal constitution* within the nation's Constitution, a form of Trojan horse.

The second section, **Recognition is not reconciliation**, contains three essays. These make clear that recognition could lead to the emergence of irreconcilable differences between Aborigines and all other Australians. James Allan argues that *recognition would hand power to judges* with unknown consequences, but at the very least be undemocratic and treat Australians unequally. Gary Johns argues that there is *already recognition enough* in Australian law and that such recognition provides instances that are harmful, often encouraging preferential treatment on the basis of race, rather than merit. Bryan

Pape prefers no change to the Constitution but confirms that it may be possible to proceed with a preamble that does not affect the interpretation of the Constitution. Nevertheless, in his opinion this would render the preamble an *irrelevant adornment*.

The third section, **A lot could, and will, go wrong**, contains five essays that outline a series of problems with, and reflections on, recognition. Wesley Aird regards recognition as *blackfella politics*, a boon to those in the Aboriginal industry but no one else. Anthony Dillon regards recognition as not only a poor means to close the gap between Aborigines and other Australians, but as having the potential to *never close the gap*. Kerryn Pholi observes that intermarriage between Aborigines and others is very high, and provides a likely scenario whereby recognition risks *upsetting the intermarriage applecart*. Frank Salter provides a comprehensive menu of *six recognition traps* that exist among known proposals, and Dallas Scott pleads with his Aboriginal colleagues and fellow travellers to *stop fighting a war already won*.

The fourth section, **International follies**, contains three essays. It provides clear evidence recognition of native peoples in national constitutions has created a number of damaging unintended consequences. Tom Flanagan retells the events of *constitutionalising Canadian Aboriginal rights* and David Round explains that *neo-tribal elites want more from New Zealanders*. Kerryn Pholi and Gary Johns argue that there is, in those nations that recognise native rights and characteristics, a large gap between recognition and treatment in *great constitution, shame about the nation*.

Questioning Aboriginal culture

1

Myths of Aboriginal cultural continuity

Ron Brunton

We ask you to teach our people to live in the Modern Age, as modern citizens ... Why do you deliberately keep us backwards? Is it merely to give yourselves the pleasures of feeling superior? ... The natural tendency of the Aboriginal is to lose his native culture and assume the culture of those associated with his uplift ... Whether the white man likes it or not, every native is headed toward the culture of the white man.

These sentences come from separate writings of John Patten, William Ferguson and William Cooper in the late 1930s. These men were the Aboriginal radicals of their day, and the main organisers of the 'Day of Mourning' protest timed to coincide with the nation's sesquicentenary celebrations in 1938. As the historian Russell McGregor has observed, what they were decrying was 'not the coming of European civilisation to Australian shores, but the fact that Europeans had selfishly attempted to exclude Aborigines from the benefits of that civilisation'.

William Cooper, in particular, argued strongly against the proposals of contemporary anthropologists who were advocating special measures to preserve the cultures of Aborigines who still felt bound by their traditions. Cooper wanted to see all Aborigines 'uplifted' into 'full British culture', and wrote that only 'compulsion so complete as to be impracticable' could force Aborigines to live 'the life of their fathers'.

In April 1938 *Abo Call*, the monthly newspaper of the Aborigines Progressive Association, carried a detailed report of the 'Day of Mourning' proceedings and speeches. Over one hundred Aborigines from the eastern states attended, and supporting telegrams and letters were received from around the country. None of the speeches, nor the ten point program for Aboriginal rights presented to Prime Minister Joseph Lyons a few days later, spoke of protecting or encouraging traditional Aboriginal cultures or laws in any way.

Embarrassment to progressive sensibilities

These earlier attitudes should give pause to those who speak of the 'continuing cultures' of Aborigines, and who want to see some form of cultural recognition in the Constitution. But today, although Patten, Ferguson and Cooper are justly praised for their struggles to achieve equality for Aboriginal people, their views about traditional cultures are an embarrassment to progressive sensibilities. In recent years, the intellectual climate has become increasingly skeptical about the cultural achievements of the West, and those who see Western civilisation as unquestionably superior to the cultures of any tribal people are derided. So why complicate the narrative about past Aboriginal heroes?

While the general disdain that Cooper and his Aboriginal comrades felt for traditional cultures is occasionally discussed in academic works, it is very rare to find these views considered elsewhere. They are certainly not mentioned in the *Recognising Aboriginal and Torres Strait Islander Peoples in the Constitution: Report of the Expert Panel* for instance, even though its 'Historical Background' chapter discusses the 'Day of Mourning' protest and its background and outcomes.

Nevertheless, apart from some remote regions where commitment to ancestral laws did continue, during the 20th century most Aborigines were following the path suggested by the progressives of the 1930s, and increasingly turning their back on traditional cultures and obligations. It was not until the 1970s – and in some areas even later – that the cultural revival whose consequences are manifest today took hold amongst significant numbers of Aborigines.

Although this revival is currently misrepresented as demonstrating cultural continuity over most of Australia, it largely drew on fragments of stories or events older people remembered from their childhood, written accounts of early observers, and the knowledge and practices of Aborigines from remote areas. Insofar as the massive loss of traditional indigenous culture is now admitted – and despite the overwhelming evidence, this is not always the case – it is invariably explained in terms of dispossession, demographic collapse and pressures from government agencies and missionaries.

Certainly, in many areas external forces undermined the capacity of Aborigines to carry out traditional observances, particularly in the early devastating years of contact with European society. But such forces constituted much less than the whole story. Substantial cultural loss was not just characteristic of regions intensely settled by Europeans. It also occurred in many areas where Aborigines were able to maintain contact with their ancestral country, and where circumstances would have enabled them to continue practicing their traditions, had they so desired.

Without ritual observances the Dreamtime is hollow

Although the centrality of what Westerners classify as the 'religious' or 'spiritual' domain to traditional Aboriginal cultures is widely recognised, this was not a matter of individual belief or faith. It was practice that was crucial – the correct performance of rituals, songs and stories; behaving in specified ways at particular times and places; and the possession of the proper knowledge required by these activities. While Aborigines may now state their firm belief in Dreamtime beings and their ongoing powers, such statements are nugatory unless the specific rituals that might be associated with such beings are observed.

Acknowledging that the voluntary decisions of Aborigines themselves played a major role in the loss of traditional practices and knowledge challenges the intelligentsia's alluring fantasies about the continuing vitality and spiritually redeeming qualities of indigenous cultures. It undermines the urgency of demands for the protection of sites whose actual or believed significance may only have been revived (Coronation Hill), or even invented (Hindmarsh Island), in recent decades, after lengthy periods of Aboriginal indifference. And it can be very damaging to many native title claims.

Successful native title applicants must establish that they are part of a society united by the acknowledgment and observance of the body of pre-contact laws and customs from which their rights to country derive. Although an unspecified degree of change can occur, the laws and customs must have continued *without major interruption* since the time of British sovereignty. Otherwise, native title is permanently lost.

Legally speaking, the reasons behind significant discontinuities in traditional laws and customs are irrelevant. Nevertheless, in my experience with native title cases, applicants often attempt to explain such discontinuities as the result of coercion or constraints imposed on Aborigines by white society. Such explanations enable the applicants to invoke arguments that, in the face of white hostility, traditional customs and beliefs were concealed, and thereby continued despite all the apparent evidence to the contrary. 'Undergrounding', as it was called, and legitimised by the anthropologist Peter Sutton in a National Native Title Tribunal publication, would clearly be very difficult to accept if it was Aborigines themselves who were primarily responsible for breaks in traditional observances and the loss of cultural knowledge.

I may be wrong, but suspect that the political push to include 'respecting the continuing cultures' in the Constitution is at least partly motivated by a desire to achieve more favourable native title outcomes, and to create a more sympathetic climate for heritage protection claims, many of which are fanciful.

Apathy, rebellion, and the withholding of knowledge

In the words of the anthropologist Basil Sansom, 'gerontocratic polygyny was the beating heart of social organization' in pre-contact Aboriginal society. Youngish bachelors might anticipate a favoured old age when they too could have multiple wives and power over younger men through their control over both the supply of marriageable young women, and the rituals and revealed knowledge that were a prerequisite for social manhood. But Europeans and the *pax Australiana* allowed the short-circuiting of this process. Hard as it might be for today's intelligentsia to accept, Europeans and their institutions provided more than just attractive new stimulants, foods and technologies. They could also offer new opportunities for freedom for both young men and women. They could allow them to avoid grueling initiation rites and forced marriages, and new ways of relating to the world, such as Christianity, however great the mismatch between European ideals and their actual application to Aborigines.

Well over a century ago, even in areas sparsely settled by Europeans, informed observers were recording attitudes and tensions within Aboriginal societies that portended the loss of significant aspects of traditional culture. In their 1899 monograph, *The Native Tribes of*

Central Australia, Baldwin Spencer and Francis Gillen wrote that in the parts of the region that had had the longest contact with whites,

> the old men see with sorrow that the younger ones do not care for the time-honoured traditions of their fathers, and refuse to hand them on to successors who, according to their ideas, are not worthy to be trusted with them.

Certainly, in a few areas there were individuals who went against the trend, and their attentiveness towards the wishes of elders and interest in the past led to them being entrusted with some information. But the processes whereby youths were ritually transformed into adults and made a party to important knowledge were collective, requiring considerable organisation and the participation of a wide range of people in particular kinship relations with the initiates. And it is clear from stories obtained by anthropologists working across Australia during the 20th century that at some time in the past, elders in many groups decided that initiations and other major customary activities should cease.

Even where initiations did continue in some form, other important aspects of traditional culture were often abandoned. In 1911, for instance, the renowned anthropologist A.R. Radcliffe-Brown spent a few weeks in the coastal Pilbara. He was given information about two hundred totemic sites in Kariera and Ngaluma country, although he was told that the seasonal renewal rituals that took place at these sites had not been performed for many years.

During the 1970s, the anthropologist Kingsley Palmer also worked in the Pilbara. Although he spent much longer in the field than Radcliffe-Brown, with his data covering a much larger area, he could identify only sixty-one totemic sites, none of which were in use, although informants said that at a few, observances had occurred until the early 1930s. External forces cannot have played much of a part in this loss. Many local Aborigines were employed in the pastoral industry, which allowed them at least some access to traditional lands, and their widespread participation in the Pilbara strike of the late 1940s suggests that the white authorities did not overly intimidate them.

In the late 1950s, the anthropologist Jeremy Beckett befriended George Dutton, an Aboriginal stockman from the north-west corner of New South Wales. Dutton was born in the 1880s and, by the time of his death in 1968, he was the last man in the region to have undergone initiation. He was genuinely interested in old rituals and stories relating to country, but found it impossible to interest the younger generation, including his own sons, in his knowledge. Writing about Dutton's life and times in the journal *Aboriginal History* in 1978 Beckett commented, 'The reader may find a certain irony in an Aboriginal turning to white people to preserve the culture which his own people were rejecting'.

Comparable examples of widespread indifference to traditional culture as against enthusiasm for Western ways, even amongst some men who had been initiated in their youth, can be found in the accounts of dozens of anthropologists writing between the 1940s until the end of the 1970s. But in the 1980s, no doubt in response to the Aboriginal cultural revival, the intellectual climate changed. The earlier anthropologists were accused of being unduly influenced by assimilationist ideas, and gullibly accepting supposed Aboriginal attempts to conceal traditional knowledge and practices and to tell white researchers only what they wanted them to hear.

Cultural revival

Such accusations are spurious, for the mid-20th century anthropologists were amongst the earliest informed critics of assimilation. The late

Kenneth Maddock made a further telling rejoinder in a fine but neglected piece on the cultural revival published in a collection of anthropological essays titled *Politics of Indigeneity in the South Pacific*. As he pointed out, those who invoke the notion of past concealment cannot evade the charge that their own research may be uncovering only what Aborigines want them to know now. And in the era of native title, with its well remunerated Aboriginal heritage and school curriculum consultants and performers, and the intelligentsia's enthusiasm for indigenous cultures, the incentives for exaggerating the persistence of traditional laws and customs are far greater than any incentives for concealment might have been in the last century.

Nevertheless, as significant as the late 20th century cultural revival seems to have been in influencing popular beliefs, enthusiasm for traditional cultural values and observances is still far from universal amongst contemporary Aborigines. Many have fully embraced the outlook and practices of their fellow Australians, and are either opposed or indifferent to the culture of their ancestors, or have an interest that is solely antiquarian. These people may be very proud of their Aboriginal identity, though without seeing it as requiring adherence to a 'distinct and unique culture'. But implicit in the arguments for cultural recognition in the Constitution is that such people can be ignored. As well as being factually misleading, a constitution that had been amended in the terms proposed by supporters of the 'Cultural Yes' case would fail the test of inclusiveness.

2

An Aboriginal constitution

Alistair Crooks

The Australian Constitution is a document that has served this country well. Its strength comes from the fact that it is minimalist, laying down only the broad structure of governance. It leaves scope for judges to re-interpret and invent to meet new challenges. It is flexible enough to deal with evolving societal mores, including the influx of immigrants from a variety of cultural backgrounds.

One aspect that is considered to be not working relates to Aboriginal affairs. Plans to change the Constitution are afoot. These proposed constitutional changes are to acknowledge the pre-existence of the 'first Australians'. It appears, however, that constitutional changes are to go much further and recognise Aboriginal culture. This proposed recognition of Aboriginal culture is, in effect, the acknowledgement of a pre-existing Aboriginal 'constitution'. There was no formal, written, constitutional document of course, but it must have existed, in a form that was sufficiently well-articulated to be the basis for a social system which was able to bind the Aboriginal people in an unchanged culture for thousands of years.

Pastor Paul Albrecht, of Hermannsburg, recognised this unwritten 'Aboriginal constitution' and its embodiment in the sacred objects or 'Tjurrunga':

> The stories of the lives and actions of the supernatural
> beings were enshrined in the myths and traditions owned

11

by the various patriclans. These stories too were known as
Tjurrunga by the Arrarnta. They were handed down orally
from generation to generation. They were said to contain the
essential 'blueprints' of life on which the people who were
the reincarnations of their respective supernatural beings
were to model their lives. In this sense the Tjurrunga can be
called the constitutional documents of Aboriginal societies.

This 'constitution', laid down by the totemic ancestors during the
'Dreaming', involved a set of rules and precedents which, bearing the
authority of those supernatural beings, were considered unchangeable
laws, which had locked Aboriginal Australians into an eternal Stone
Age. Bishop Francis Gsell, a missionary of 50 years experience, largely
on Bathurst Island in the Northern Territory, noted this rigidity:

> The word progress when applied to the aboriginal in his
> natural state is only a fetish.

Professor Peter Sutton too observed that 'the idea of social progress
comes from outside Aboriginal tradition'. Aborigines believed that the
ancestors had given them the solemn duty, through the performance
of the ancient 'increase ceremonies' using the Tjurrunga, to ensure
the very continuation of life on earth. This was a sacred responsibility
they took extremely seriously, and any deviation from Dreamtime
precedents, or in the ceremonial performances, even if accidental, put
the future of everyone in severe jeopardy. Kathleen Strehlow quotes
examples provided by her anthropologist father of the response to
accidental or deliberate acts of sacrilege:

> At the full performance of the eagle cycle of Akar Intjota at
> Uralawuraka, east of Charlotte Waters, in the 1850s or 1860s
> … All went well at this festival 'till an unfortunate accident
> one morning. This accident was deemed to constitute a
> grave act of sacrilege against the grim eagle ancestors. There

were cries of alarm from the watching men and shouts of murderous anger from the ceremonial chief and his elders. The young men involved in the accident – there were either two or three of them – were immediately seized. Their necks were twisted around till the vertebrae had been dislocated, and they were probably choked to death as well.

If the clans involved did not act, it was the duty of others to act in their place.

I have also frequently heard the remark made that if any Tjuruŋa secrets were revealed to women and children, men from outside clans would intervene and kill the offenders unless their own council of elders had first taken action. Thus, in 1949 Rauwiraka told me the story of the alleged slaughter of a whole camp of natives somewhere near Mt. Eba many years ago. In this camp the men had been in the habit of changing sacred songs and performing ritual acts in the presence of women contrary to their own laws ... The news of this sacrilege spread in the western areas from place to place, and intense fury was aroused everywhere. At last a large band of men from all sides headed for the offending district ... Man, woman, and children were slaughtered, and their bodies flung into their own fires and left to burn.

Daisy Bates described a similar massacre from Western Australia:

In a case of this kind where a camp defies its own laws, the law-keepers of the adjoining districts (all able-bodies are law-keepers in these cases) must take vengeance, and if their numbers are not sufficient, they can call in the services of natives from outlying districts, to restore the native laws which offenders such as the Ida Hill men had entirely laid aside.

This same rigidity was even enforced on a personal level, limiting the scope for individual progress and individual expression. As Bishop Gsell reported:

> Inevitably, as in all societies, outstanding personalities make themselves felt amongst their number, but this pre-eminence will confer only a limited influence and purely a moral one. And because competition raises its head here as elsewhere, this pre-eminence and moral influence do not last for long ... one day sooner or later, such a superior one will be found with an anonymous spear through his body. Why? For the simple reason that nobody is allowed to speak any louder than the others. The head emerging above the crowd is cut off. To go either more quickly or more slowly than the others is a sign of rebellion which merits severe punishment.

The Aboriginal constitution was rigid, inflexible, and non-inclusive. This was demonstrated by thousands of years without significant change, followed by collapse at the first major arrival of immigrants who came from outside their Dreaming tradition. There was no provision in the Aboriginal constitution for making changes to that constitution. It is arguable that the lack of progress in the remote communities can be traced directly to rigidity of tradition.

The question is, do Australians really want to introduce the Aboriginal constitution into the Australian Constitution? Because of the indivisibility of sacred and secular life, the recognition of traditional culture is the *de facto* recognition of an Aboriginal constitution and all the cultural rules and mores that flow from it. Is this really the intention?

Initiation rites to be rights?

For most Aboriginal boys, traditional culture effectively started at puberty with the initiation to manhood. As Greenway described in 1972, for the Arrarnta of central Australia:

> a boy becomes a man by having an upper central incisor pounded out of his head with a rock, without anaesthetic, without permission to express pain or terror; by having his foreskin cut off in little pieces with a stone knife and seeing it eaten by certain of his male relatives, and as a climax of agony, by having his penis slit through to the urethra from the scrotum to the meatus, like a hot dog.

The penis is so disfigured by the operation that the introduction to traditional Aboriginal culture for the just-pubescent girls is to be 'modified' in order to cope. As Willshire, also describing the Arrarnta in 1891, puts rather coyly:

> Commerce with the opposite sex is difficult under the circumstances [subincision], and in order to overcome the difficulty the females are subjected to mutilation of a frightful character, with a view to the permanent enlargement of the parts which are operated upon. The incisions internal and external are made with sharp stones or stone knives, and the operators are always the old men of the tribes. The exact details of the procedure are so abominable that it would be impossible to adequately to describe them in language fit for the general reader. The performance of these mutilations inflicts permanent injury upon the victims. Some of them do not survive the ordeal.

Or as Warin in 2007 less coyly quotes:

> Hole not big enough, makem bigger.

It should be noted that the old traditional practices have not disappeared from the remote communities. A recent report on child marriage launched by the National Children's and Youth Law Centre stated there was anecdotal evidence that forced child marriage occurred in some indigenous communities.

And not long before that, the *Mail Online* reported that at Borroloola, Northern Territory (23 January 2014):

> Three Aborigine boys airlifted to hospital after circumcision ritual goes horrifically wrong and they are left sitting in 'pools of blood'.

A repeat of a similar event from Tennant Creek in 2010:

> Aboriginal boys turned up in the grounds of a bush hospital on December 30. They stood outside with blood pouring down their legs … There are concerns as well that young men are being snatched by elders and forced to go through the procedure against their will.

Martin Flanagan reported in 2010 in *The Age* that 'payback', sanctioned under traditional law, is still practised in some remote communities:

> In traditional Aboriginal society, events, which cannot be explained by other means, can be attributed to sorcery. This affected the Yuendumu football team in the 2000s when an older player, a stalwart of the side, retired and his guernsey was passed to a newcomer. Great significance is attached to players' guernseys. When the newcomer to the Yuendumu team fell ill with cancer and died, the belief grew that the person responsible for the death was the player who had formerly worn his guernsey. This dispute, fuelled by alcohol, was the backdrop for the knife fight in the Alice Springs town camp in late 2010, which resulted in the death of one young man and the wounding of two others.

Are we now to elevate these practices to the mainstream by conferring the prestige of constitutional recognition? Will the vulnerable be excluded from access to equality before the law or the right to refuse to participate? The last example is most alarming since sorcery played a major role, not only in determining the identity of the allegedly guilty party to be the subject of payback, but that a crime had been committed in the first place.

Yet, the Law Reform Commission's Report on the recognition of Aboriginal traditional law (1986) appears to indicate that there is support for the recognition of customary practices, both in the Aboriginal communities, and amongst some in the legal profession.

In the words of a senior Aboriginal community worker with a State Department of Community Welfare:

> Aboriginal Customary Law which is still recognised and practised in traditional areas today is the same law which has been handed down from generation to generation and it must be recognised and respected by the Law Reform Commission.

The Commission found consistent support among Aboriginal people for the basic idea of recognition of Aboriginal customary laws. It concluded that there were good arguments for recognising Aboriginal customary laws, including 'the need to acknowledge the relevance and validity of Aboriginal customary laws for many Aborigines.' Similarly, the 2012 Report of the Expert Panel, *Recognising Aboriginal and Torres Strait Islander Peoples in the Constitution*, shows support for 'respecting culture' of which customary law is one vital component. Their preferred wording in the constitutional recognition includes 'respecting the continuing cultures, languages and heritage of Aboriginal and Torres Strait Islander peoples'.

Perhaps more importantly, the report authors appear to argue that constitutional recognition is just one step towards a greater place for customary law in the governance of Australia:

> Nor should constitutional recognition in general have any detrimental effect, beyond what may already have been suffered, on future projects aimed at a greater place for customary law in the governance of Australia.

Their agenda is clear. It would be foolish to pretend it did not exist. Would any Australian respect the rite of sub-incision or payback? To respect these, as part of a continuing culture, is to fly in the face of what evolving enlightenment has achieved over a thousand years of progress.

Recognition is not reconciliation

3

Recognition hands power to judges

James Allan

There are two ways to understand disagreement on important public issues. One way is to assume your own view is the result of some pipeline to God, indisputably good in other words, and so all those who disagree with you are either dumb, malevolent or in need of re-education.

The other way is simply to recognise that a lot of smart, nice, well-informed people simply disagree on all sorts of important issues. These may range from euthanasia, to how to deal with those trying (dare one say illegally?) to come to Australia by boat, over to labour relations, on to whether to amend our Constitution, and more.

Notice that on this second understanding of disagreement the obvious way to resolve issues is to count everyone as equals and vote, a process otherwise known as democracy. As to the first way to understand disagreement, it rests on the rather implausible premise that, by some cosmic fluke, your moral and political antennae quiver at the perfect frequency – you are the pinnacle of moral evolution – while people who disagree with you are somehow substandard.

Change is not self-evidently good

I start by mentioning this because almost all that I have read on amending the Constitution, to insert a recognition clause, seems to be premised on the view that change is self-evidently good and that opponents either need to be re-educated, or exposed for the racists they are, or some combination of the two.

But that is plain out bunk. And it is bunk whether it comes from the left of politics (as in the past) or whether it now comes from the right of politics.

First off, let us be clear that writing and amending a constitution is not a matter of the heart. It is about producing a document that will stand the test of time and that (in my view) will allow democracy to flourish so that our children and grandchildren can make decisions for themselves. And that is a matter of hard-nosed calculation with more than a little cost-benefit analysis. It is not a matter of emoting or tugging at the heart strings.

Let me turn to this issue of constitutional change. To start, you need to realise that Australia is one of the oldest democracies on earth. Yes, our young nation has been a democracy – a successful democracy – longer than all but a half-dozen or so other countries on earth. And that is in part because the Constitution we have is, in my view, the best written constitution on the planet. We copied much from the United States, most obviously their version of bicameralism and federalism, and then we made ours better than theirs by flat out rejecting a judge-empowering bill of rights.

We also opted for a Swiss-style amending provision. That means that if you wish to amend the Constitution you have to ask the voters. You cannot by-pass them and amend it by just getting most of the politicians to agree, as is the case in the US and Canada. Think about that and ask yourself if Australia would still be a constitutional monarchy if constitutional amendments were wholly up to the political class.

My larger point, though, is that what we have 'sure as heck ain't broken'. And that, for any sensible person, is something to consider when people push for change.

Inventing interpretations

There is a more crucial second consideration. In the last two decades or so our top judges have taken to interpreting our Constitution in a way that I think is very hard to defend. Twenty years ago the High Court discovered, or read in, or flat out made up (according to taste), an implied freedom of political communication. I count myself as one of the biggest free speech adherents in the country, and in substantive terms, I like this outcome. But, as a matter of honestly interpreting the words of the Constitution, these cases strike me as so implausible as to be laughable.

And in a democracy where all of us count equally, with an equal vote to choose people to make social policy, that is a very bad thing. It makes it very hard to trust the top judges to read the document in the way it was clearly intended by those who framed it. Whatever the clear intentions of the drafters, the words might be given any meaning that the point-of-application judges happen to find in keeping with their vague sense of what are prevailing social values or ethos.

Consider a couple of recent voting rights cases in which the High Court, in my view, issued two of the least defensible and most interpretively implausible decisions I have read since coming to this country a decade ago. In both instances, the High Court over-ruled the elected Parliament and struck down statutes passed by the elected representatives of the people.

And they did so, in my view, with virtually no textual warrant from the Constitution and in clear opposition to what those who framed the words actually, and with next to no doubt, intended. The top judges treated the words as some sort of jumping-off point for seeing the Constitution as a 'living tree' that can be pruned and altered over time. But, of course, that re-shaping can only be done by them, seven unelected ex-lawyers.

My point here is wholly independent of whether or not you like the substantive outcome of these cases. Remember, I very much like the outcome of the implied freedom cases. Yet, being able to rely on a plausible and an honest approach to interpretation – one that leaves the last word on all big-ticket social issues with the elected representatives of the people – is simply more important.

Once you go down the road that our top judges have detoured onto, it becomes something of an unknown how a change to the Constitution today will be treated by a future High Court in 15 or 20 years. Change, today, carries big risks down the road, because what we intend the new words to mean today becomes more or less irrelevant to how they will interpret them in the future.

Let me be frank. I am an ardent adherent of letting the numbers count and democratic decision-making. I fear that latter day judges might use any mooted recognition clause in the Constitution to do things unimaginable or pooh-poohed today.

If you doubt that, ask yourself how many people at the start of the 1900s thought that the phrase 'directly chosen by the people' could be used by judges to dictate when the electoral rolls could close (the *Rowe* case), or that some of those in prison could vote when Parliament said they could not (the *Roach* case). The answer is none of them thought this. They thought they were leaving these issues to the Parliament.

So when people today assure you that the words they propose

to insert will transfer no power to our unelected judges, there is a strong basis for being sceptical, at least until we see what explicit words emerge as the proposed amendment – and even after that. Remember, as with all democracies, ours has an independent judiciary, which is a very good thing indeed. But it also means that it will not be the Prime Minister or Attorney General who will be interpreting these provisions in the future. It will be judges. Assurances by the Prime Minister and the Attorney General that the proposed words will be taken to mean X or Y, or will have minimum impact, are simply worthless. When Canada amended its Constitution in 1982 the top judges did not just ignore the meaning of provisions that had been stated by the top politicians, they explicitly said it was of no account. They overruled it.

So let me put this as politely as I can. Not only am I doubtful that anything nearly explicit enough to begin to reassure me will emerge about the wording of any recognition clause, I even worry that the seemingly-reassuring-enough will not prove constraining-on-the-judges-enough in the long run.

New Zealand is cause to pause

Alas, there is a third reason for scepticism regarding any proposed constitutional recognition change. I spent 11 years teaching law in New Zealand. In many ways, I loved the place. But to hear some proponents of this constitutional amendment point across the Tasman to the Treaty of Waitangi over there, and to do so as some model we ought to copy, frankly beggars belief.

Here is a small taste of what has happened in New Zealand, in the name of this short little three-clause treaty. First off, the judges there have simply invented a 'partnership' principle – they have decreed that there is some partnership between the Crown and Maori. Then there is talk of 'Treaty principles' though no one honestly has the slightest idea what this one page document signed in 1840 has in the way of principles. This, of course, is not a problem if your goal really is to treat the document as a springboard to 'read-in' the desires of today's metropolitan elite.

And then there are all the race-based divisions it has fostered in New Zealand. And there are the weird divisions between tribal and city Maori and the endless 'final settlements' that never prove final. And there is the way that it fosters rent-seeking behaviour to benefit the tribal elite far, far more, than the poor in cities.

Put bluntly, the renewed emphasis on the Treaty in New Zealand has undermined democracy. At least that is my view. And it seems bizarre to me that proponents of change in Australia would want to hold up New Zealand as a model to emulate. I fear this change would undermine democracy in Australia too.

That said we could obviously keep an open mind on this particular issue until we see the proposed wording of any mooted change to the Constitution. But let us be clear and honest. There are solid, powerful and democratically motivated grounds for being very leery of this suggested constitutional change.

Modest changes may be harmless

The other likely amendments, by contrast, seem to me to give few if any grounds for concern. If there is a desire to repeal section 25, the 'provision as to races disqualified for voting', then that is fine by me. The section is defunct in all practical senses and explicitly removing it affects nothing. If that symbolism were desired, I would vote to satisfy such a desire.

Meanwhile, the Commonwealth's race power in section 51 (xxvi) is no doubt more complicated, for at least two main reasons. One is that this section was altered in 1967 by constitutional referendum, to delete an exemption about 'the aboriginal race in any state'. Post the 1967 referendum the Commonwealth was no longer exempted from making laws for Aborigines if, as a group, such laws fell within the 'people of any race for whom it is deemed necessary to make special laws' s.51 (xxvi) head of power. But the scope of that power remains unclear.

Hence, the second complication is that a straight repeal of s.51(xxvi) has federalism implications and would leave this power wholly with the States. So any s.51(xxvi) change that was aimed at a 'status quo but with better symbolism' outcome would need a repeal plus a replacement. That could work. I would vote for it if worded properly. But it will be tricky.

All in all, then, we can see that playing with 'symbolism' is as tricky as playing with fire. You had better be very careful indeed. And you would like to think that those interpreting the instructions had a defensible approach to interpreting the words they were reading.

4

Already recognition enough

Gary Johns

Mick Dodson has argued that if the Australian Constitution is to have any relevance to Aborigines and any enduring relevance to Australian society, it has to 'affirm our basic identity as human beings'. What a magnificent contradiction. Aborigines are not human beings, Dodson asserts, unless the Constitution recognises them. The Constitution mentions no one else, so presumably all Australians are not human beings. The inflated language of recognition is matched only by the absence of logic.

Aborigines and Aboriginal culture are well recognised in Australian law. There are acts of parliament dealing with solely Aboriginal matters, such as native title and heritage, and in other legislation to ensure that Aboriginal culture is taken into account. Such recognition, however, has created a number of problems. First, Aboriginal culture is sometimes used to seek priority over others. Second, it is rarely defined, which makes it difficult to oppose. Third, where culture is defined, the acceptance of some Aboriginal behaviour as 'cultural', risks allowing behaviour that would otherwise not be tolerated. Fourth, Aboriginality has become problematic, and when authorities require proof of Aboriginality, for example, to grant a benefit, the evidence may be unconvincing.

Sensitivity in referring to Aborigines is indicative of the barriers that have been erected between Aborigines and others in these times of Reconciliation. Commercial radio codes, for example, provide guidelines on the portrayal of 'Indigenous Australians' or 'Aboriginal People'. The code makes clear that the word 'Aboriginal' is an adjective used to describe something associated with an Aborigine, the noun. It cautions, however, that Aborigine is not a popular term. Of course, indigenous is derived from the Latin 'indigena' meaning 'native', which is also no longer a popular term. Recognising Aborigines in the Constitution will make these sensitivities more intense. Recognising Aboriginal attributes, such as culture, will deepen the problems that exist with the present level of recognition.

What is Aboriginal culture?

Aboriginal leader Noel Pearson recently described a common cultural practice in Aboriginal society – 'demand sharing' or 'humbugging'. In the vexed issue of the right to alcohol, Pearson stated, 'The ideal position is that we don't have alcohol in Aboriginal communities because alcohol and strong kinship don't mix, they drink until nothing is left'. Aborigines demand the right to be treated like others, but also the right to be protected from others. Which right should win?

Cultural 'safety' is the latest fashion in the Aboriginal industry. A research report of the Victorian Aboriginal Childcare Agency, *This is Forever Business: a framework for maintaining and restoring cultural safety in Aboriginal Victoria*, is a prime example. Aboriginal culture is nowhere defined in this report. Nowhere, is there proof that, when 'saved', Aboriginal culture will lead to any discernible difference to the lives of Aborigines. Nowhere, is it made clear, apart from funding Aboriginal-run organisations, what benefits flow in providing cultural safety.

The logic of cultural safety, and Noel Pearson's need to protect

Aborigines from grog because of culture, is that Aborigines must choose to either live in a self-imposed exile, using the money of others, or break free. Which is it that constitutional recognition seeks to deliver: protective custody or freedom?

The struggle over the problematic nature of Aboriginal culture has been long. The West Australia Supreme Court sentenced Aboriginal natives, Boynjat and Wobut, to death in 1849 for killing a native boy, Injerwert. Police gave evidence that each had been warned in the past not to spear other natives. Through interpreters, each made a confession:

> Wobut: The deceased was connected with a man who caused by magic death of my brother. I speared the deceased, rather a slight wound, but if it had not been for the other natives present, I should have killed the deceased myself.
>
> Boynjat: I speared the deceased in the leg, because Wobut's brother was my relation.

The Coroner reported:

> Examination of the body of the deceased revealed ... a large orifice under the left shoulder, below it looked as if a spear or other weapon had been worked about in the wound; one of the ribs was also broken; the vertebrae appeared as if there had been some violence to that part; there was also a punctured wound on each side above the groin, and another on the upper part of the left thigh. I have no doubt that the deceased met with a violent death.

Aborigines had been warned for many years to desist with their cultural practices, and yet as late as the mid 1980s members of the legal profession, expressed through law reform commissions, wanted to recognise Aboriginal culture, including pay-back and tribal punishment. Both are unacceptable in the wider society.

Access to children

Aborigines and their culture are well recognised, if not well defined, in Australian law. In the matter of parenting orders, the *Family Law Act 1975* (Cth), states that the child has a right 'to enjoy his or her Aboriginal culture', including the right to enjoy that culture with other people who share that culture. Such recognition creates difficulties.

Should a child of Aboriginal descent, for example, spend more time with his Aboriginal father or more time with his sibling, the child of his non-Aboriginal mother? This dilemma faced a Family Court judge in Sydney, in 2012 (*Jerome & Tanzer*). The Aboriginal father lived in the Blue Mountains west of Sydney, to all intents and purposes, in the suburbs. He wanted attention and weight given to his heritage. No consideration was given to the mother's heritage. The court decided that the child should live with the mother, to bond with a new sibling and visit the father on the weekends for 'culture'. At present, courts are able to take such matters into account. Should the Constitution, however, include Aboriginal culture, the freedom to do so may be curtailed to the detriment of others.

Aboriginal adoption

Sensitivities in the adoption of Aboriginal children are especially acute following the Stolen Generations episode. The provisions of the *Adoption Act 1984* (Vic), recognise the principles of Aboriginal 'self-management' and 'self-determination' and make the dubious assertion that 'adoption is absent in customary Aboriginal child care arrangements'. These ideological statements are used to justify the transfer of a large degree of power from the state to Aboriginal agencies.

The Act determines that, for example, where a parent who is an

Aborigine gives consent to the adoption of a child and wishes the child to be adopted within the Aboriginal community, the parent should receive counselling from an Aboriginal agency. If an Aboriginal person is not available to adopt, proposed adoptive parents may be approved by an Aboriginal agency.

Where a parent consents to the adoption of an Aboriginal child, the adoption order may be made subject to the condition that a parent or the parents, relatives of the child and members of the Aboriginal community to which the child belongs, have a right to have access to the child.

Constitutional recognition may make the placement of children, in their best interests, more difficult.

Burying the dead

Coroners and Coroner's Courts have the unenviable task of deciding who has the right to choose the place of burial of a relative. In the Supreme Court Victoria action, in 2012 (*Carter v Coroners Court of Victoria*), a sister of a deceased woman wished to take her sister's body to be buried at Lake Tyers in Victoria. The Chief Executive Officer of the Dandenong & District Aborigines Co-Operative Ltd wrote to the Coroners Court and advised that the traditional country of the deceased was Gunai/Kurnai at Lake Tyers Reserve and that it would be culturally appropriate to return the body of the deceased to Lake Tyers Reserve for burial on her traditional country.

The trouble was that the woman did not wish to be buried at Lake Tyers among her own. Shortly before her death, she wrote, that, 'I wish to be cremated and don't want to be buried on Lake Tyers … [rather, to] be put near our foster parents at Bunurong Cemetery.' Foster parents raised the deceased woman from the age of six and were considered by her as her real parents.

The *Coroner's Act 2008* (Vic) ensures that different cultures, which have different beliefs and practices surrounding death, should, where appropriate, be respected. The case was determined on the basis of the better claim, in this case the hierarchy of claim was in favour of the de facto husband and against the sister, but the lesser claims of the Aboriginal community were heard. Constitutional recognition may lend weight to lesser claims, those of Aborigines, to whom this woman of Aboriginal origins owed little allegiance.

Sentencing criminals

Too many Aborigines are in gaol because too many Aborigines commit crimes. On the issue of proof, Australian courts must treat all those who come before them, including Aborigines, in exactly the same manner. The same does not apply in sentencing. Each Australian State has a penalties and sentences regime. The *Sentencing Act 1995* (WA), for example, directs the court to take into account those factors that 'decrease the culpability of the offender or decrease the extent to which the offender should be punished'.

In 2010, Ernest Munda of Fitzroy Crossing in Western Australia killed his common-law wife of 16 years, with whom he had four children. He was sentenced to prison for seven years and nine months, with a non-parole period of three years and three months.

Taxpayers funded an appeal to the High Court that his sentence was too harsh. He claimed that the Court of Appeal of Western Australia failed to have 'proper regard' to his personal circumstances as a 'traditional' Aboriginal man. In particular, 'an environment in which the abuse of alcohol is endemic in indigenous communities', was not taken into account.

The High Court knocked him back. The court reiterated that

while a person's background could play a part in mitigation, it needed to be 'weighed by the sentencing judge'. At present, judges have discretion, but in the future, if Aboriginal culture is recognised in the Constitution, the likes of Ernest Munda may receive lighter sentences.

Proof of Aboriginality

An applicant for an Aboriginal benefit, such as a housing or business loan, Abstudy and special assistance, or the waiver of school or TAFE fees, on most occasions, has to produce evidence of Aboriginal lineage, or a certificate from a land council, or a statutory declaration.

The widely accepted definition of an Aborigine means a person who:

- Is descended from an Aborigine.
- Identifies as an Aborigine, and
- Is accepted as an Aborigine by an Aboriginal community.

The Commonwealth Education Department, for example, 'may require students, or parents/caregivers or providers on their behalf, to sign a statutory declaration' stating that the students are Aboriginal. In some instances, where a person's status is challenged, the department may require a person to demonstrate their descent and/or acceptance by an Aboriginal community. In an environment where governments are desperate to have as many 'Aborigines' succeed as possible, there is no incentive to check veracity.

The institutions least likely to seek proof are universities and schools, who are desperate to sign up students for boasting rights, and funding, which comes with each student. It does not pay them to pay close attention.

Each Aboriginal applicant for an Indigenous Business Australia loan must complete a statutory declaration. The statutory declaration requires the applicant to state 'that he or she is of Aboriginal descent, *some* (emphasis added), or all of the applicant's ancestors must be Aboriginal people'. It is interesting that IBA requires some, not just one, ancestor, despite the convention that any ancestor is supposedly enough to make one an Aborigine.

Where proof counts, in voting or a dispute between Aboriginal groups, matters can become fraught. Native title claims, for example, often pit one group of Aborigines against another. In a recent case, the judge observed with some displeasure that statements made by the claimant group 'had been structured and expressed under the guidance of a common hand' (*Bidjara People v State of Queensland 2013*). A Federal court found that two candidates for the regional Aboriginal and Torres Strait Islander Commission election, who had been challenged by other candidates, were not Aboriginal (*Shaw v Wolf 1998*) because of insufficient proof of descent.

Aborigines are recognised in Australian law. There may be some benefit in this, but there are considerable problems in doing so, not least, the incentive to make unwarranted claims, to seek unwarranted priority, and to cheat for benefits. Constitutional recognition will not improve the benefits, but they will strengthen the incentives to do wrong.

5

Cosmetic preamble an irrelevant adornment

Bryan Pape

When it is not necessary to change; it is necessary not to change
(Lucius Cary, 2nd Viscount Falkland 1641)

When in 1900, the United Kingdom Parliament passed the *Commonwealth of Australia Constitution Act*, there was a preamble to the Act, but there was no preamble to the Constitution itself as set out in section 9. This chapter contends that a preamble to the Constitution remains unnecessary on three grounds. First, historically, second, that it would be irrelevant to its purpose and third, that it would be of no help in its interpretation.

As to the first ground, reference is made to a few salient events from Australia's time as a self-governing independent colony, to its independence as a nation state. In short, from British subjects to Australian citizens. As to the second ground, it is contended that a preamble would be irrelevant to the organs and machinery of a federal system of government. Finally, if a preamble were to be included, it would serve no useful purpose as an aid to the judicial interpretation of the Constitution. In other words, it would only serve to mislead.

The first ground – historical

Why was a preamble unnecessary? When the Commonwealth of Australia came into being on 1 January 1901, it was as an independent self-governing colony of Great Britain. Six self-governing colonies federated as the Commonwealth of Australia for defined and limited purposes. Then, the Governor-General was the representative of the British Government responsible to the Secretary of State for the Colonies and the Colonial Office as was the case with the State Governors.

Historically, the idea of a preamble to the Constitution itself seems to have not been contemplated, for the simple reason that it could add nothing to what was already said in the preamble to the Act. There, the words, 'under the Crown' were of special importance. Quick and Garran, in their *Annotated Constitution of the Commonwealth*, noted:

> This phrase ('under the Crown') occurs in the preamble, and is not repeated, either in the clauses creating the Commonwealth or in the Constitution itself. ... It is a concrete and unequivocal acknowledgment of a principle which pervades the whole scheme of Government; harmony with the British Constitution and loyalty to the Queen as to the visible central authority uniting the British Empire with its multitudinous peoples and its complex divisions of political power.

Federation to World War II

Having suffered horrific casualties in World War I (1914-1918) with 65 per cent of total embarkations becoming casualties, (including 58,961 killed and 166,811 wounded out of a population in 1918 of five million), Australia, along with other Dominions sought to gain their independence from Great Britain.

The Imperial Conference of 1926 and the Balfour Declaration were the catalyst for the drafting of the Statute of Westminster at the

Imperial Conference of 1930 and its passing by the United Kingdom Parliament on 11 December 1931. One of the Balfour Declarations provided that the Governors-General of the Dominions would no longer act as representatives of the British Government.

When then did Australia become a nation state? The *Statute of Westminster 1931* (Imp) gave the Dominions their independence from Great Britain. The *Colonial Laws Validity Act 1865* (Imp) now had no application to the Dominions. It had provided that if a colonial law was repugnant to an English law, which applied directly to the colony, then it was void and inoperative. Australia was reticent, if not reluctant to adopt it. Many in the Commonwealth Parliament seemed to prefer the colonial status.

What Prime Minister Robert Menzies said on 3 September 1939 seemed to accord with the view of Australia's colonial status when in a radio broadcast he said:

> ... it was his melancholy duty to inform you officially, that in consequence of a persistence by Germany in her invasion of Poland, Great Britain has declared war upon her, and that, as a result, Australia is also at war ...

Contrastingly, after the Japanese attack on Pearl Harbour and Malaya on 7 December 1941, King George VI acting on the advice of Prime Minister John Curtin, and on 8 December, through the Governor-General, declared war on Japan. This was the act of an independent nation.

The Second World War brought an end to the colonial relationship. Singapore fell to the Japanese Army on 15 February 1942. Having escaped from the Philippines, United States General Douglas Macarthur arrived in Australia on 17 March to become the Supreme Commander of Allied Forces South West Pacific.

There too were the fierce and decisive battles of the Coral Sea in May and Midway Island in June. Co-incidentally, 'the Battle' on the validity of the supposedly temporary Uniform Tax legislation was fought in the High Court in June.

On 9 October 1942, the Commonwealth Parliament passed the *Statute of Westminster Adoption Act 1942* (Cth) retrospectively to the outbreak of war against Germany on 3 September 1939. For the Statute of Westminster to extend to the Commonwealth of Australia, it was required to be adopted by the Parliament. In my view, Australia became an independent nation on 3 September 1939. Its adoption had the legal effect of confirming the 1939 and 1941 declarations of war as acts of an independent nation.

Post World War II to the Australia Act 1986

Soon after the end of World War II in 1945, the Minister for Immigration, Arthur Calwell initiated a great immigration program to bring many people to Australia from the United Kingdom and Europe. Some found work in the massive Snowy Mountains Hydro Electricity Scheme.

On 26 January 1949 the *Nationality and Citizenship Act 1948* (Cth) (later renamed as the *Australian Citizenship Act 2007*) came into force. Persons born on or after that date were Australian citizens by birth, before then persons born in Australia had the status of British subjects but became Australian citizens under the Act.

This change gradually ushered in a new era in the way Australians saw themselves as seen by the passing of the *Flags Act 1953* (Cth), in which the blue Australian National Flag was formally adopted. The Australian Aboriginal Flag was appointed and proclaimed under the Act in 2008 to be recognised as the flag of the Aboriginal Peoples of Australia.

The second ground – the organs and machinery for a federal system of government

The preamble to the *Commonwealth of Australia Constitution Act* (Imp) states:

> Whereas the people of New South Wales, Victoria, South Australia, Queensland and Tasmania … have agreed to unite in one indissoluble Federal Commonwealth under the Crown of the United Kingdom of Great Britain and Ireland, and under the Constitution hereby established:

'To unite in one indissoluble Federal Commonwealth' points to what follows in the Constitution. Its chapters set out the organs and machinery of a federal government under the Westminster system. The powers and rules for administering the three arms of responsible Government, the Parliament, the Executive and an independent Judiciary are set out in Chapters I, II and III respectively. They are followed by Chapter IV which deals with Finance and Trade, Chapter V which covers the States and the overlooked Chapter VI which provides rules for the creation of New States. Chapter VII deals with the seat of Government and with the excision of the Australian Capital Territory from New South Wales and finally, Chapter VIII deals with the rules for the alteration of the Constitution. To put not too fine a point on it, the Constitution is a rule book to regulate the relationship between the Commonwealth and the States.

Lord Hopetoun, the first Governor-General, swore in the first Executive Council of seven members on 1 January 1901 at a ceremony held in Centennial Park in Sydney. Edmund Barton, conventionally then known as the Prime Minister, was sworn in as Minister for External Affairs. The Duke of York (later King George V) opened the first Parliament in Melbourne on 9 May 1901. It sat

in the Victorian Parliament House until 9 May 1927, when the Duke
of York (later King George VI) opened the new Parliament House in
Canberra. In 1903 the then peripatetic High Court of Australia sat for
the first time, with Sir Samuel Griffith as Chief Justice with Justices
Barton and O'Connor. Appeals then lay to the Privy Council, other
than for constitutional questions between the Commonwealth and
the States unless permitted by the High Court. These appointments
enlivened the Constitution.

Contrasted with the limited and definite powers of the
Commonwealth Parliament were the indefinite powers of the State
Parliaments preserved by section 107 of the Constitution, so now
glaringly ignored by Canberra.

Appeals to the Queen in Council which formerly lay from the High
Court were restricted by the passing of the *Privy Council (Limitation
of Appeals) Act 1968* (Cth) and were effectively abolished by the
commencement on 8 July 1975 of the *Privy Council (Appeals from the
High Court) Act 1975* (Cth). Chief Justice Murray Gleeson in a 2008
paper to the Anglo-Australasian Lawyers Society in London noted,
'until the 1968 legislation took effect, the Privy Council heard income
tax appeals' (for example, *McClelland v Commissioner of Taxation 1970*)
in which the Privy Council reversed the High Court. Chief Justice
Gleeson went on to note the contribution that the Privy Council had
made:

> For a substantial part of the 20th century, Australia saw itself
> as part of the British Empire, later the Commonwealth of
> Nations, and *the idea that the common law might vary throughout
> them was barely contemplated.* (My emphasis)

Earlier Chief Justice Owen Dixon, with the concurrence of the
other members of the High Court in *Parker v Queen* (1963) stated in

relation to whether the Court should follow decisions of the House of Lords said:

> I think it forces a critical situation in our (Dominion) relation to the judicial authority as precedents of decisions in England. Hitherto I have thought that we ought to follow decisions of the House of Lords, at the expense of our own opinions and cases decided here, but having carefully studied Smith's Case (1961) I think that we cannot adhere to that view or policy.

All of this led to Chief Justice Garfield Barwick's 1977 restatement of the High Court's position with respect to the House of Lords and also that 'in future (it) would not regard itself as bound by decisions of the Privy Council.'

Privy Council appeals from the Supreme Courts of the States were not finally abolished until 1986.

Essentially the Constitution is about federalism but it cannot properly be understood without reading the *Statute of Westminster Adoption Act 1942* (Cth) and the *Australia Act 1986* (Cth).

The final ground – no aid to interpretation

The general common law rule is that a preamble to an Act does not form part of the Act and as such is disregarded in its interpretation. With respect to the interpretation of Commonwealth legislation, the preamble is now treated as part of the Act, by s.13(2)(b) of the *Acts Interpretation Act 1901* (Cth).

Similarly, if the Constitution were to be altered by inserting a preamble it would form part of the Constitution and as such could be used as an aid to interpretation, unless it was specifically provided that the preamble was to be disregarded. This was the case with the lapsed *Constitution Alteration (Preamble) Bill 1999* (Cth).

If a preamble were to be added to the Constitution, it is doubtful that it would serve any useful purpose because of the inherent subject matter of the Constitution, namely a rule book for a federal system of government. It would be like mixing oil with water.

Conclusion

The insertion of a preamble to the Constitution would be to misconceive its very purpose in establishing the organs and machinery for a federal system of government. To tack on a cosmetic preamble would be an irrelevant adornment. Let the Constitution speak for itself.

A lot could, and will,
go wrong

6

Recognition is blackfella politics

Wesley Aird

There is merit in amendments to the Constitution to replace racially discriminatory provisions. It might also be appropriate for the proposal to include a succinct statement that Aboriginal and Torres Strait Islander peoples were the original inhabitants of present-day Australia. It is highly inappropriate, however, to attempt to use the Constitution to promote indigenous culture or to promote one group over the rest of the Australian population. Such an attempt would almost certainly jeopardise the chances of success of the referendum and could be expected, quite rightly, to fail.

With only minor amendments, the Constitution has retained its character even though it was written a long time ago when society was very different. There have been minor updates on select matters to bring the document into line with prevailing norms as Australian society and economy have matured. Since the first referendum in 1906, Australian voters have approved only eight out of 44 propositions. In the main, the eight are not remarkable, and it seems constitutional amendment is acceptable for what may be termed, technical refinement, for example, Senate elections (1906) and Senate casual vacancies (1977), retirement of judges (1977), and referendums (1977).

Proposals that have gone to the spirit or intent of the document, or that may have appeared as a major social shift, have usually failed.

The Republican referendum of 1999 comes to mind. An exception was the successful 1967 referendum, which made explicit powers for the Commonwealth to deal with Aboriginal matters.

Against this change-averse backdrop presently there is apparent bipartisan political support for a referendum to recognise indigenous people in the Constitution. Although a national conversation on the concept has been going for some years, the proposed wording to go to vote will not be known before late 2014.

In the rhetoric and popular media the recognition campaign has a 'feel-good' element to it. Australians are told that recognising indigenous Australians in the Constitution will achieve many things, ranging from 'completing' the document to uniting the nation, and many things in between. But a referendum is not only a popularity contest. Usually, it is a very specific proposition that may have consequences, both known and unknown, at the time of the poll, and for many years thereafter.

Unknown consequences

In December 2010, the Australian Government appointed the Expert Panel on Constitutional Recognition of Aboriginal and Torres Strait Islander peoples with Professor Patrick Dodson as Co-Chair. In support of the campaign he states:

> Recognition of the first peoples in the Constitution sends a message that Australians value Aborigines, that they are important, that they are respected, and we want to deal with the things that have caused us division and discord in the past.

In this statement, the Co-Chair of the Expert Panel quite reasonably points out there is a feel-good element. He goes on to suggest, however, that there may also be consequences that are unknown. There is no way of knowing, for example, how 'the things that have caused us division and discord in the past' are to be dealt with. Perhaps it may be by an individual emotional experience – but that does not require an amendment to the Constitution. Given that a referendum is a specific proposition with specific consequences, perhaps it is envisaged the past is dealt with by having two types or classes of citizens (indigenous and non-indigenous) recognised in the Constitution. If successful, this may open the door to preferential race-based services even if it looks and feels like positive discrimination for the specific purpose of overcoming indigenous disadvantage. Such an approach would certainly appeal to many indigenous people, and their supporters, seeking to deal with the things that have caused 'division and discord in the past' by some form of transaction or compensation, even if it is delivered by an indirect means.

The Constitution is a solemn document of the greatest importance for all Australians and must not be capable of being used by one group seeking advantage or leverage over others. Programs that are predominantly social in nature tend to be funded in boom times. When the Commonwealth Budget is in deficit, however, taxpayers rightly expect to see value for their money. Therefore, in lean times, programs that do not deliver results are at greater risk of being cut.

The Australian Government's *Indigenous Expenditure Report* is a recent initiative to gauge expenditure on services to indigenous Australians. Only two editions have been produced so far; the first in February 2011 and the second in September 2012. The 2012 *Indigenous Expenditure Report* found the ratio of indigenous to non-indigenous expenditure per head of population was 2.99:1 in school education; 4.89:1 in public and community health services; and, 4.85:1 in housing. The indigenous population is younger than the mainstream population, and there are greater levels of disadvantage across the indigenous population, so it is reasonable to expect higher expenditure in health and housing. If the higher expenditure were achieving results, however, it could be argued to be worthwhile. Senior government ministers think otherwise.

The Prime Minister's 2014 *Closing the Gap Report* suggests indigenous affairs may be ready for change:

> In too many areas, people's lives are not improving or not improving fast enough … We should not equate spending money with getting results. Spending more money on indigenous Australians is not a sign of success and is not something that should be celebrated for its own sake.

Aboriginal people are very good at helping part government from its taxpayers' money. For decades, there has been a steady flow of money from the government to indigenous communities and individuals through a bewildering array of programs and grants. Results, in many, but not all cases, have disappointed. Where programs or grants have been initiated for specious reasons, not only is it a wasted opportunity, but also most likely it raises the expectation on the part of the recipient that more money will follow.

From the *Indigenous Expenditure Report* and the *Closing the Gap Report*, it is plain that the indigenous expenditure has reached levels that are difficult to sustain without solid evidence of improvements across the range of social indicators. With government budget savings to be found, it is no surprise senior government officials refer to our times as 'the end of the age of entitlement'. There is a very real possibility there will be cuts to indigenous programs, including some that have been around for quite some time. The indigenous industry will need to seek alternative means of income, and it is not out of the question that some are looking to constitutional recognition to provide extra leverage to extract money from government.

If certain individuals or groups require assistance from government to overcome genuine disadvantage then this is reasonable, and assistance should be provided on the same terms and with the same obligations that apply to other Australians. There should be no special help from the Constitution. The Constitution is not the place to 'deal with the things that have caused us division and discord in the past.'

It may sound a little ludicrous to suggest, as I have, that there is a risk that a section of the community might attempt to use the Constitution to extract money from government. It may even sound paranoid to attempt to draw a line from the Constitution to the indigenous industry, however, as Joseph Heller wrote in Catch 22, 'Just because you're paranoid doesn't mean they aren't after you.'

Who is or is not

One of the great values of the Constitution is its equal treatment of all Australians. It is a document for all citizens regardless of race, culture or origin. Any attempt to set apart indigenous Australians is problematic because of the uncertainty regarding identification.

In recent times, governments have relied on a three-part identification for indigeneity: these relate to genealogy (or descent), self-identification and acceptance by an indigenous community. Where a person seeks to identify as indigenous for the purpose of accessing a government or economic benefit, this approach makes sense. Where identification is simply for an individual's sense of belonging (that is, nothing hinges on the answer), the three-part question becomes somewhat less relevant. The better educated or, the more a person participates in the economy, the lesser that person needs to identify as indigenous.

The personal or social nature of unreliable identification is manifest in the process of our periodic census. The Australian Bureau of Statistics reports that, from the 2011 Census, there were 19,900,764 non-indigenous, 548,369 indigenous people and 1,058,586 'status not stated'. The 'status not stated' is quite remarkable as this census question was not optional. On census night, there could be (quite literally) a million reasons for a person leaving blank a response for whether or not he or she is indigenous. But that is approximately half 'indigenous' as 'not stated'.

With such an extraordinary difference between the numbers of 'indigenous' versus 'not stated' it seems wrong to put so much faith in the quantum of a half million or so indigenous Australians. It would be honest to admit that the number of indigenous Australians is simply unknown. By extension, special status or privileges cannot reasonably be conferred upon such an amorphous group.

Some more equal than others

The Constitution was conceived, drafted and approved by Australians to provide the basic rules for government and, as such, binds everybody even if, in the hundred plus years since federation, the cultural mix of 'everybody' has changed significantly. It is reasonable to assume its authors had intended the document would treat all Australian citizens equally. At the time, at the Constitution's origin, 'equal' was not as universal as might be expected today, and so in the spirit of modern inclusiveness the Constitution ought to be brought up to date by minor amendment to replace racially discriminatory sections.

It is also reasonable, as a matter of historical fact, to make a succinct and plain statement that prior to settlement the continent was inhabited by Aboriginal and Torres Strait Islander peoples. Anything more than a simple statement of historical fact risks the process being jeopardised by 'blackfella politics'. The national appetite for indigenous symbolism has so often led office-bearers awry and, in many instances, high profile indigenous individuals have misused significant public events for self-aggrandisement. To allow this mischief to extend into the Constitution would be a calamity on the grandest of scales.

It is reasonable for an amended Constitution to mention Aboriginal and Torres Strait Islander peoples but only at this highest level of identity or cultural affiliation. It would be counter-productive for the Constitution to name sub-groups (that is to name specific groups of people by geographic region, cultural or language affiliation). Firstly, it would create inequality within the indigenous citizenry (insofar as it is known) on the basis of the groups that get a mention and those that do not because a value judgement would be made by which some groups would be legitimised and other groups would be ignored. The effect would be to categorise winners and losers by some expert panel and this would be open to challenge. Secondly, there would be inequality within the broader national citizenry, again on the basis of cultural groups that get a mention and those that do not.

Subjective or romantic statements about indigenous culture are not appropriate for the legislation that sets out the rules by which all are governed. This is not the place for cultural agendas or campaigns. To have any chance of success in achieving a double majority at the polls, the propositions must be unreservedly consistent with the tenor of the document.

Conclusion

A referendum is a specific legal proposition with specific consequences. Whilst the opportunity to replace racially discriminatory sections should be embraced, the risks of unintended consequences are real. Interest groups must not use the Constitution as leverage to further their particular interests.

Beyond technical amendment with a historically accurate statement, the chances of a successful double majority for the referendum are already starting to look bleak.

7

Recognition may mean
never closing the gap

Anthony Dillon

I need to start by describing what this chapter is not about. In the hypersensitive, politically correct climate in which we live, it is sometimes necessary to commence this way. When discussing Aboriginal matters there seems to be no end to where offence can be taken and accusations of racism made. This chapter is not about opposing the proposition that Aboriginal people be recognised as Australia's first people, nor is it about preventing Aboriginal people from embracing, practising, or celebrating what could be considered Aboriginal 'culture'. I respect Aborigines' right to practice their culture - so long as it is within the confines of the ordinary law of the land. Further, I do not oppose constitutional amendments that are intended to help prevent racist practices. In line with the theme of this book, however, I have some concerns regarding the recognition of Aborigines and their culture in a document that carries legal weight. There is potential ambiguity regarding what 'blanket' recognition will mean and its implications.

The views expressed in this chapter reflect my current thinking on what is a complicated matter. While I have my opinions on the topic, they are not as firm as my views on other topics – topics to which I will draw links in this chapter. My thinking leans towards, 'If it ain't broke, don't fix it'. The assertion that 'it ain't broke' will draw criticism. Some will argue that with the 'gap' as wide as it is, with all the inequities of poor health, poor education outcomes, high incarceration rates, something is certainly 'broke'. Some will make the leap from 'it is broke' to 'recognition in the Constitution will fix it'. Please explain to me the logic in that?

Should Aboriginal people be recognised in the Constitution?

Some Aboriginal people suffer greatly, that needs addressing, but there is also a huge and growing number who enjoy success. These latter include more than 30,000 university graduates, sports heroes, politicians, artists and musicians, business people, and unsung heroes (like the ordinary people paying off their mortgage who are fine contributors to their communities). All of these people have achieved what they have without constitutional recognition. How? I would suggest simply by following the same formula for success as most other Australians who have achieved success: do not segregate yourself from society; treat others with respect and see them as equals; pursue an education (whether it be formal or informal); make valuable contributions to the community in which you live; be a role model for others to emulate; make healthy choices; and adhere to a personal moral code. So when thinking about how best to address the problems facing Aboriginal people, is it really necessary to have some formal recognition of Aboriginal people any more than we recognise other racial/cultural groups in Australia? I am questioning whether recognition will be the catalyst to improvement: I am not necessarily opposing it.

Many of those Aborigines active in the Constitution debate are themselves very successful. It is my desire that all Aborigines have the same degree of success which the Aboriginal people I refer to have been able to achieve without recognition in the Constitution. I realise there will be some who believe that recognition is not about fixing problems, but about doing the right thing. Aboriginal people were the first people on this continent and all Australians should know this basic fact. Recognising in the Constitution that Aborigines are the first Australians is fine. There is a small risk, however, that some will see this as the 'magic bullet' to fix all problems. Much like Kevin Rudd's apology (which I never opposed but did not believe would achieve what many wanted), there was a great expectation of 'healing'. It did not bring healing, only short-term relief to some and hope to others. Anyone who derived any lasting benefit very likely did so because they realised that healing comes from offering forgiveness, not from pursuing an apology.

I am not saying that Aboriginal people should not be recognised in the Constitution as Australia's first people. Perhaps it might be worthwhile making the necessary amendment to at least 'give it a go'. If acknowledgement contributes either directly or indirectly to solving the problems many face (poor health, unsafe and unclean living conditions, violent and dysfunctional communities, unemployment, low educational attainment), then I will happily admit that I was wrong and will join in the celebration that we have made some progress in closing the gap. If it does not contribute towards solving problems, however, then maybe the failure to see any improvement in the lives of Aborigines may help us focus energy where we are likely to get a greater return – education, employment, and ready access to the sorts of services most of us take for granted. In sum, I am suggesting we need to think carefully about whether acknowledging Aboriginal people in the Constitution will help close the gap.

Should Aboriginal culture be recognised in the Constitution?

With regard to recognising Aboriginal culture in the Constitution, I have stronger reservations. Will the recognition of Aboriginal culture (one that is assumed to be, by definition, radically different from non-Aboriginal culture) highlight commonalities between two races, or will it further entrench the differences where they may exist and create more differences where they do not exist? Is it possible that recognising Aboriginal culture in the Constitution will be seen as another magic bullet? When any initiative is seen as a magic bullet, there will be less emphasis on what individuals and communities can do to solve problems, and greater expectation on what the magic bullet can achieve.

My concern that changes to the Constitution will be seen as a magic bullet is based on my observation that so many seem to believe that an acknowledgement of past injustices committed against Aborigines at, and since the invasion, is the magic bullet that will fix the problems we see today. To those holding such a view, I simply say, 'nonsense'. Acknowledging injustices of the past is fine, but insisting that others also acknowledge these injustices is not the solution for problems facing many Aborigines today. In fact the insistence on acknowledgement distracts us from finding real solutions. I am simply suggesting that some people expect that amendments to the Constitution will achieve more than what they can legitimately be expected to achieve.

When discussing the recognition of culture, there is the problem of deciding exactly what is Aboriginal culture. Is it living off the land, telling dreamtime stories, undergoing tribal initiations, spearing offenders in the leg, or simply just a feeling? Or is it tautological in nature? Is it whatever someone who identifies as Aboriginal decides it to be? With regard to those who claim to have 'Aboriginal culture', I have (generally speaking) met three types of people. The first group are those who genuinely have elements of it as evidenced by the language spoken, daily living practices, beliefs, the goals they pursue, and their general outlook on life. They are clearly distinct from non-Aboriginal Australians. The second group are typically well adapted mainstream Aussies who have their own personal way of embracing Aboriginal culture, which typically amounts to beliefs, identification, attitudes, and sometimes speaking (parts of) a traditional language. They value their Aboriginal ancestry, are comfortable in themselves, and have no need for others to acknowledge their cultural expression. I have such a friend who always greets me in the traditional language of his and my Aboriginal ancestors in a way that is both beautiful and genuine.

The third group are those who insist that they are fundamentally different to other Australians and have needs vastly different to other Australians - though typically they accept useful and rewarding aspects of modernity. Perhaps they seek to convince others because they need convincing themselves? Some from this group appear to be virtually indistinguishable from people with no Aboriginal ancestry. They regularly demonstrate dissatisfaction with life, non-Aboriginal people, and the (white) government. They believe that the cause of their dissatisfaction is the gulf of cultural difference between them and non-Aboriginal Australians. The solution therefore, in their opinion, is different rules and laws to cater for the perceived cultural differences they loudly and insistently proclaim. To borrow a term used by a colleague, Brian Roberts, I call this group 'culture vultures'.

Culture vultures

There are many beautiful aspects of traditional Aboriginal culture – family values, respect for nature, sharing and caring (also shared with other cultures) – that I believe make this world better. The expression of living one's culture does not appear to be hindered by a lack of recognition in the Constitution. Further, the many thousands of happy, successful Aboriginal people, who are flourishing despite the lack of constitutional recognition of culture, are surely evidence that such recognition is not needed. I think those who demand constitutional recognition of culture do so for similar reasons to those who demand a treaty – it is an attempt to further validate their Aboriginality, by constructing an 'us' and 'them' division. Such validation is only needed if one lacks the internal conviction of one's Aboriginality.

Those with the us-and-them mentality tend to speak about 'sovereignty' (but rarely articulate what it actually is), are quick to insist that anyone who is without Aboriginal ancestry is guilty of living on stolen land, and believe that those who are entitled to call themselves 'Aboriginal people' (that is, anyone with any Aboriginal ancestry, no matter how minimal) are owed rent from 'them' (the non-Aboriginal Australians; the descendants of the invaders; the 'new arrivals'; the 'boat people'). Such a mindset I think flies in the face of the true traditional Aboriginal mindset of oneness, interconnectedness and unity.

Recognition of culture in the Constitution has the potential to open the gate to different rules for people with Aboriginal ancestry and become a 'lawyer's picnic'. One very concerning example of different rules is the insistence on placing children in need of short-term and long-term care with 'culturally appropriate' carers. Currently, for children with Aboriginal ancestry (however minimal) the Aboriginality of potential carers is given far too much weight. This practice has sometimes ended in tragedy. Some children have suffered, all in the name of 'culture'. A colour-blind culture or way of life, characterised by love is a far more important consideration than a culture that is assumed to be Aboriginal simply because the adult potential carers themselves have some Aboriginal ancestry.

Finally, let us not forget the obvious elephant in the room – who is an Aborigine? Currently, anyone with any Aboriginal ancestry is entitled to identify as an Aboriginal Australian. This generous criterion is aligned with the ridiculous mantra, 'You are either Aboriginal or you are not'. Categorising Australians as Aboriginal, or not, by these rules contributes to the emergence of 'Aboriginal experts' who act as gatekeepers and significantly influence the national discussion on Aboriginal affairs. As a consequence of the stridency of these 'expert voices' (some of whom only discover their voices in the later stages of their lives), discussions are monitored and controlled to the point where non-Aboriginal people are constrained in expressing their opinions on matters that affect their fellow Australians. Some are not game to open their mouth because so many of these gatekeepers loudly proclaim that non-Aboriginal people have no right to have or to express an opinion on these matters. This 'us-vs-them' separatism lines the pockets of a few but keeps many Aboriginal people from reaching their full potential.

My gravest concern is that recognising culture in the Constitution has the potential to accentuate the us-vs-them divide. Even more dangerously, privileging Aboriginal culture with the full force of the law has the potential to spark a 'feeding frenzy' of 'culture vultures', an endless welter of ever more strident demands for special consideration. Perhaps my concerns are unfounded, but I suggest that we need to think it through very carefully. We need to ask ourselves: will changing the Constitution put food on the table, get kids into school, adults into jobs, and families living in safe, clean environments?

8

Upsetting the intermarriage applecart

Kerryn Pholi

Do we need the grand public gesture of 'constitutional recognition' to close a supposedly painful divide between Aboriginal and non-Aboriginal Australians? The rate of growth of Aboriginal intermarriage suggests the two groups have been busily reconciling privately for quite some time. Rather than healing a rift between us, the creation of separate Aboriginal cultural rights and entitlements in the Constitution has the potential to poison relationships within many Australian families, and could drive us further apart than we have been for generations.

Intermarriage is normal

Australians of Aboriginal descent and those without any Aboriginal ancestry clearly get along well enough to live together, sometimes get married to each other, and to make babies together. In the urban and regional centres where most Aboriginal people live, intermarriage is the norm, not the exception. The children produced by these partnerships are, in a statistical sense, 'Aboriginal', because to be *statistically* Aboriginal one must simply be 'of Aboriginal origin', meaning one has some Aboriginal ancestry. When the children of these mixed partnerships grow up and have children of their own, the offspring will also be 'Aboriginal', regardless of the heritage of the other partner involved, as will their offspring in turn. While this convention creates a rate of Aboriginal population growth that causes headaches for statisticians, one could argue that it is a clear sign of progress in practical reconciliation. Not only are increasing numbers of ordinary Australians willing to claim their Aboriginal ancestry, but plenty of ordinary Australians of various origins are also participating in the business of making more Aboriginal people. As the product of such a mixed partnership myself, I regard this form of practical, do-it-yourself reconciliation a very good thing.

An Aborigine defined

In the legal sense, 'an Aboriginal person is an individual of Aboriginal descent who identifies as an Aboriginal and is accepted as such by the community in which he [or she] lives'. In other words, a person with a claim to Aboriginal ancestry, and who 'feels like' an Aboriginal person, and who is accepted as such by some other people, is an Aboriginal person in the eyes of the law. A person of Aboriginal descent may have spent a lifetime 'feeling like' an Aboriginal person, or they may decide, in the light of whatever legal or administrative matter is at hand, that an 'Aboriginal person' is what they have always felt themselves to be. The third requirement, that the individual be accepted as an Aboriginal person by the community in which he/she lives, is also open to creative interpretations of the meaning of both 'acceptance' and of 'community'. In short, a legal claim to Aboriginal identity is based upon an individual's genetic inheritance and the narrative he or she chooses to weave around it.

At present, Aboriginal people make up around three per cent of the Australian population. As the Aboriginal population continues to grow, and as recognisable features of Aboriginal 'origins' become increasingly dilute, an individual's Aboriginal identity may in time come to be regarded as unremarkable or inconsequential and largely irrelevant. While some – myself included – would accept such a development as another very good thing, others may consider it a threat to existing race-based rights and entitlements, and may seek to create a more exclusive legal definition of Aboriginality.

A number of people have pointed out the problems that will arise with the creation of constitutionally enshrined rights or entitlements for a 'racial' group that is both growing rapidly and becoming increasingly difficult to delineate. The inclusion of clauses that pledge 'respect for Aboriginal cultures, languages and heritage' and acknowledge 'the need to secure the advancement of Aboriginal peoples' could create conditions in which a person with a long-ago Aboriginal ancestor may, in certain situations, find it legally advantageous to cultivate a claim of Aboriginal identity. They could also create a flattering narrative surrounding this identity, and exaggerate its significance to the legal issue in question. Critics of the proposal for substantive constitutional change have pointed out that separate provisions for Aboriginal cultural rights in the Constitution may lead to inequality before the law in criminal cases, in administrative matters concerning benefits, grants and other special provisions, and in civil cases concerning aggrieved and 'offended' Aboriginal plaintiffs.

For some voters, the potential for such legal inequities would be enough to dissuade them from supporting constitutional recognition of Aboriginal cultural rights. Supporters of constitutional change, however, may reason that any descendants of the dispossessed 'first Australians' deserve some compensation, even if they now live in conditions of reasonable prosperity. They may reason that compassionate Australians should be willing to collectively bear any costs of compensation and gestures of 'respect' for Aboriginal culture. They may further reason that it matters not if some people take unfair or undeserved advantage of such entitlements if other, more needy Aboriginal people, are helped in the process. There is a possibility that Australians will vote for the inclusion of Aboriginal cultural provisions in the Constitution, not because they recognise a specific need, but because it seems like a nice, mostly harmless gesture that may even do some good for some Aboriginal people.

That Aboriginal issues are exclusively Aboriginal people's business is a misguided belief. Well-meaning, non-Aboriginal Australians are satisfied to make apologetic gestures, endorse the provision of government funding, oppose 'assimilationist' interventions, and for the most part, respectfully stay out of Aboriginal affairs. The implications of the legal inequities, discussed above, may be of little interest to voters who have no intention of becoming engaged in the criminal justice system (either as an offender or as a victim), do not intend to compete against Aboriginal applicants for a job, a grant or other such benefits, and do not intend to voice any public opinions that may be offensive to Aboriginal people. Such voters may feel insulated from any risks inherent in the proposed constitutional changes. After all, what risks could these changes possibly present for well-meaning, respectful, culturally sensitive, law-abiding and decent Australians?

To answer this question, I should firstly summarise some pertinent points:

- Partnerships between Aboriginal and non-Aboriginal people are commonplace.
- 'Mixed' partnerships produce children that can legally be regarded as 'Aboriginal'.
- Unfortunately, mixed partnerships, like other relationships, do not always work out, and
- Relationship breakdowns can lead to acrimonious disputes over access to children.

A hypothetical case

The recognition of Aboriginal cultural rights in the Constitution presents risks to any and all Australian families, because the intermarriage trend suggests that any Australian family could at some stage include some Aboriginal people. This means that any Australian family could find itself in dispute with an Aboriginal family member. Here is a hypothetical scenario to help illustrate the nature of the risk:

> You are the proud parents of a very nice young man. Your beloved son meets a lovely young woman, who happens to be of Aboriginal descent. They marry, and together they produce your grandchildren, whom you, naturally, adore. Time passes: things go well, then things go badly, your son and daughter-in-law decide to divorce, and then things go to court and become ugly. The now *emphatically* Aboriginal mother of your Aboriginal grandchildren wishes to relocate – for 'cultural' reasons. To support her claim, she invokes her right as an Aboriginal mother to ensure her children's continuing connection with their culture and heritage. Furthermore, she claims that her in-laws (that is you) are undermining and disrespecting the cultural legacy she, as an Aboriginal mother, is obligated to pass on to her Aboriginal children. It is her preference that your access to your grandchildren be significantly restricted, in the interests of protecting the cultural wellbeing of her (Aboriginal) children.

If this scenario sounds far-fetched, perhaps you are unfamiliar with the intensity of bitterness and spite that a custody dispute can induce in otherwise decent and reasonable people. If you feel that the hypothetical Aboriginal mother is an unrealistic character, I will counter that I might behave in a similar manner if I found myself in her position. I am a person of Aboriginal descent; if it were to be written in the Australian Constitution that my 'advancement' should be secured and that my culture and heritage should be respected, why would I hesitate to invoke these entitlements in order to get something I desperately wanted?

Perhaps an expert in constitutional law will scoff that the proposed 'reforms' are intended to establish a commitment to action at the macro level of government policy and the allocation of resources and that they would not be applicable at the micro level of disputes in the Family Court. We are yet to see, however, any clear assurances around the limitations of these proposed cultural rights and entitlements. Besides, what self-respecting lawyer would hesitate to cite my 'constitutional rights' as an Aboriginal person, however dubious, if there was a remote possibility that this would lend support to my case?

If our national Constitution could potentially be invoked to bolster the claims of Aboriginal parents over the conflicting claims of their non-Aboriginal partners, how might this impact on the day-to-day business of parenting in a 'mixed' partnership? What will it be like to co-parent Aboriginal children, when one parent becomes more legitimate than the other in the eyes of the law? Even with the best intentions of both parents, such an imbalance of power may be corrosive to a healthy relationship, and toxic in one that is problematic.

Should changes to the Constitution provide the means for an Aboriginal parent to assert his or her cultural rights and entitlements over the wishes of other family members, the prudent course of action for non-Aboriginal Australians would be to avoid entangling themselves in relationships with Aboriginal people. Put simply, having children with an Aboriginal person would suddenly become a risky prospect. Non-Aboriginal grandparents and other in-laws would be wise to tread carefully, lest they offend the cultural sensitivities of the Aboriginal parent - however arbitrary or rudimentary these 'sensitivities' may be. Partnering a person who does not express any particular interest in his or her Aboriginal heritage carries risk, as a reinvigorated claim of Aboriginal heritage may become a weapon to be wielded in the event of a dispute. As a precautionary measure, some Australian families may choose to subtly inculcate their young people against any interest in forming social relationships with Aborigines, in order to prevent the formation of an ill-fated partnership.

Fewer mixed partnerships

Should Aboriginal cultural rights become part of the Australian Constitution, it may produce some interesting effects in the Aboriginal population. We may see a reduction in the number of 'mixed' partnerships, as non-Aboriginal Australians may conclude that the imbalance of power such partnerships entail is simply too dangerous and demoralising. This would slow the rate of Aboriginal population growth, and would also maintain the 'purity' of Aboriginal bloodlines (for those whose bloodlines were 'pure'), as the scope of potential partners would narrow to others within the Aboriginal population. Differences in both physical appearance and social norms between Aboriginal people and 'white' Australians would remain, to the extent they are, recognisable. The legal and statistical definitions of Aboriginality would then make sense in ways that they had before intermarriage became an acceptable practice. As a result, claims to distinct and separate Aboriginal legal rights - perhaps even a treaty - would become more feasible. Emerging differences in social norms and values may make it difficult for Aboriginal and non-Aboriginal Australians to live and work harmoniously together, therefore, separate

Aboriginal industries, institutions and enclaves may be required.

It is no mystery why nostalgia for 1967 infuses the campaign for constitutional change; it represents a return to a simpler era, where everybody knew their place and kept to their own kind. Should this sad, sick vision of our retrograde future become a reality, rest assured that there will be plenty of highly skilled Aboriginal professionals and cultural experts available to manage the separate industries, institutions and enclaves, and to liaise on behalf of their Aboriginal charges with the 'white' world outside. Who are these future leaders of the Aboriginal apartheid? Start finding out at www.recognise.org. au.

9

Six recognition traps

Frank Salter

Prime Minister Tony Abbott has stated his intention of holding a referendum to recognise indigenous Australians in the Constitution. The referendum questions have not been announced so it is impossible to praise or criticise their wording. It is appropriate, however, to warn the framers and the public about likely pitfalls, especially when it appears that the Coalition Government is unaware of all the traps awaiting them. Evidence for this is the Government's taking seriously the *Report* of the Expert Panel appointed by the Gillard Government. The Coalition has not accepted the *Report's* recommendations, but neither has it condemned them, more than two years after they were released, despite the *Report* being riddled with traps for good government, social cohesion and national sovereignty.

One snare the Coalition is unlikely to step into is to place recognition clauses in the legally-binding body of the Constitution, as recommended by the *Report*. Indications are that the Government prefers the safer location of the Preamble. Also, the Government is unlikely to propose the Orwellian prohibition of 'racial discrimination', also recommended by the Gillard Panel, which Tony Abbott described as a backdoor bill of rights. The proposed section 116A would bar government from discriminating on the basis of ethnicity except for providing special services to disadvantaged populations, such as Aborigines. This would assist the human rights industry to obstruct policies intended to manage indigenous affairs, border protection and immigration. Promoting anything like 116A would be such an obvious failure of prudence and such a betrayal of Coalition voters and the citizenry as a whole, that it is unthinkable that parties calling themselves Liberal or National would commit such a blunder.

My guess is that the Government will limit reliance on the *Report* to the seemingly innocuous recommendations to recognise indigenous prior habitation in the Preamble, add some other words of acknowledgement, and delete one or more sections from the body of the Constitution. Unfortunately the *Report* formulates these proposals in hazardous ways.

As a result there are six traps in the *Report* awaiting the Government.

TRAP #1: Ethnic bias

The constitutional recognition movement seeks unilateral recognition of indigenous Australians. This would be ethnically biased because it would omit the British pioneers and settlers, their institutional traditions and their Christian religion and folk culture that laid the foundations of the nation. The omission is unprincipled because the reason given for recognition – that it would acknowledge the country's origins – also applies to the pioneers. Omitting or downplaying the British role in founding the Commonwealth would be a gratuitous insult to the great majority of Australians. It is, after all, the nation's Constitution. The Australian nation created the Commonwealth to serve its collective needs. In that sense the Constitution belongs to the nation, as its instrument.

The symbolism of excluding the nation from its own Constitution would deal a blow to social cohesion and sovereignty. It would establish, in the founding document, the prejudicial 'Acknowledgement of

Country' ceremony that is routinely imposed, unrequested, on school assemblies and other public meetings. That ceremony would be acceptable if it acknowledged the cultural identity of the pioneers and the nation's sovereignty over all of Australia's lands and waters. But in its present form – essentially what is being proposed for the Constitution – it implies that more than 97 per cent of Australians have an inferior status: that the population apart from Aborigines and Torres Strait Islanders are interlopers, recent arrivals who have not acquired ties or rights to the land.

That would undermine social cohesion because multicultural societies depend on the majority population feeling sufficiently secure in status and belonging that they do not feel threatened by demographic and cultural change. The privileged recognition of indigenous peoples would undermine the majority's sense of security in two ways. First, it would call into doubt the territorial bond that is an essential component of national identity. Second, it would tend to provoke nationalist resentment among non-indigenous Australians, increasing the risk of polarisation between them, indigenous peoples and immigrant minorities.

In the larger view it would be improper for the Australian Government to call into doubt the nation's sovereignty. And the bedrock of sovereignty is the nation's undivided and unqualified possession of Australian territory, bestowed upon it by the colonising power, Britain, but more fundamentally earned by the sweat and tears of building the nation from a wilderness. Recognising indigenous peoples is consistent with national sovereignty but not if those peoples are attributed a claim to Australia that competes with the nation's possession of it.

Asking voters to approve such a provision would not only lay a trap for the nation. It would also expose the Coalition Government to the humiliation of a no vote, which would be a real possibility if Australians came to realise the injustice of their own Constitution being turned against the memory of those who wrote it. The humiliation and political losses that resulted would be well deserved.

TRAP # 2: Requiring equal outcomes

The *Report* proposes these words for the Constitution: 'Acknowledging the need to secure the advancement of Aboriginal and Torres Strait Islander peoples'. Such words would be dangerous, even if placed in the Preamble. The Gillard Government shied away from this open-ended provision and the Abbott Government is unlikely to put these words in the referendum. Equivalent words might be offered, however, such as requiring governments to achieve equal outcomes, to close the gap separating indigenous Australians from the remainder of the population. Tony Abbott has stated his belief in equal outcomes. To demand that outcomes be equalised not only in health and school attendance but also in broad socio-economic measures, would burden Australians with guilt and extra taxes for the foreseeable future.

Pro-recognition advocates claim that recognition would go a long way to closing the gap. The evidence suggests otherwise. According to the Productivity Commission, Australian governments in 2011-2012 spent more than double per person on services for indigenous citizens than on other citizens. An equal outcomes provision in the Constitution would mean that this massive subsidy would be judged insufficient if the gap did not rapidly close.

Recognition will do nothing at all for Aboriginal income or health that does not involve extracting more taxes and other concessions from the rest of the population.

TRAP # 3: Land-grab by circumventing Mabo

The *Report* recommends acknowledging indigenous peoples' 'continuing relationship . . . with their traditional lands and waters' and 'continuing cultures, languages and heritage'. For many, perhaps most Aborigines, these are false claims. Yet they would possess the authority of the Constitution. It is inevitable that this authority would be used to reinterpret the High Court's Mabo ruling of 1992, which laid down the conditions under which indigenous communities gain land rights. The Mabo ruling made native title conditional on applicants demonstrating continuity of the laws and customs that tie them to the land in question. This has been a thorn in the side of the native title applicants. A constitutional declaration of continuity, even if patently false, would likely widen and intensify claims to native title, and would advance the goal of carving an Aboriginal nation out of the Commonwealth. It would further undermine national legitimacy.

Inspiration for this recommendation came from the 2007 United Nations Declaration on the Rights of Indigenous Peoples, rejected by the Howard Government but signed by the Rudd Government in 2009. This is an ideologically extreme document which, in several places, conflicts with the United Nations Convention on the Elimination of All Forms of Racial Discrimination to which Australia is also a signatory.

A treaty would be another way to circumvent Mabo. The *Report* did not propose a provision empowering or requiring the Commonwealth government to treaty with its own citizens. However, Warren Mundine, chief indigenous adviser to the Prime Minister, has urged the Government to negotiate treaties with indigenous groups. This would override the Mabo provisions as assuredly as would asserting continuity of culture and ties to the land. Voters should decline any referendum proposal that advances that agenda.

TRAP # 4: Designating indigenous languages 'national heritage'

The *Report* recommends designating all indigenous languages 'national heritage'. This could have legal, financial and perhaps legitimacy consequences, for example, if governments are legally bound to preserve these languages or teachers to instruct school children about them. The lack of a sunset clause means that all indigenous languages would remain privileged no matter how many speakers used them. The wording put to voters should be carefully chosen to avoid liability. The *Report* also recommends designating English as the 'national language', which is insufficient recognition. If native languages with only hundreds, and sometimes dozens, of speakers are officially to be made part of the national heritage, surely English is a much larger and more fundamental part. English should be recognised as the founding national language and protected as the common idiom of the law and government.

TRAP # 5: Change of the race power

The *Report* recommends that section 51(xxvi) be repealed. This section authorises Parliament to legislate with respect to 'The people of any race for whom it is deemed necessary to make special laws.' Repeal of this section would impede governments' ability to direct policies at particular ethnic groups, which they must do in some circumstances, mainly to provide for the special needs of indigenous peoples. Most of those uses have been affirmative, that is, the provision of extra services. Unsurprisingly, this has not attracted accusations of discrimination. However, the Howard government's Intervention in the Northern Territory in 2007 was affirmative only with regard to the children it was intended to rescue from neglect and sexual abuse. It was, as it needed to be, a military and police action directed explicitly at Aboriginal communities. To undertake this policy the Howard

Government exempted the Intervention from the *Racial Discrimination Act 1975* (Cth), a manoeuvre that attracted considerable criticism and would have been impossible if the Constitution had prohibited differential treatment of ethnic groups, as proposed in section 116A.

Repealing section 51(xxvi) is touted as removing the race power. In fact, the *Report* recommended substituting one race power for another specified in the proposed section 116A. This change would take much discretion out of the hands of Parliament. The new power would favour minorities while the existing provision promotes flexible government, in effect favouring the majority and minorities as need arises.

The repeal is also meant to remove the word 'race' from the Constitution, an explicit recommendation of the Expert Panel, which judged it outdated. To do so without substituting alternatives would spring another trap because it would neuter the Constitution with regard to this important dimension of human identity and biodiversity. 'Race' as used in the Constitution is the term used before World War II to designate descent groups larger than the clan: ethnicity, nation and physically distinct populations. This breadth means that the term retains validity if interpreted with an eye to its meaning at the time the Constitution was written.

The *Report's* case against the existing race power and 'race' was based on a combination of cultural Marxism and ignorance, a disappointing combination in an Australian government commission. It was also due to a pronounced ethnic bias against white Australia and not only in the proportion of panel members. Most of the minority members had a track record of advocating their ethnic interests but none of the Anglo members did. Ethnic balance in numbers and loyalty might seem a quaint notion in a multicultural society where the majority is routinely excluded from the policy table. But it would have been fair to include majority voices in a high level commission that was deliberating matters that will impact the ethnic interests of indigenous and non-indigenous Australians alike.

TRAP # 6: No sunset clauses

The special rights recommended by the Gillard Expert Panel – to recognition, advancement, land and language protection – have no expiry dates or conditions. This means that governments would be forced to continue extraordinary levels of support for indigenous Australians, whether or not in need. The Aboriginal industry would become a fixture. Failure to include sunset provisions would violate the provisions of the United Nations Convention on eliminating racial discrimination, to which Australia is a signatory. It would also be dangerous to make expiry conditional on equal outcomes because ethnic groups often differ in preferences and performance even when opportunities are equal.

Conclusion

It is to be hoped that the Abbott Government recognises the yawning traps in the *Report* and the animus or indifference to the Australian people that they bespeak. Any constitutional changes should be proofed against impeding representative government or harming national cohesion or sovereignty. To that end no agenda should be served apart from historical recognition. That would help make the amendments function as a final settlement, the end of the reconciliation process instead of the basis for new demands on national identity, taxpayers and landholders. Above all, if the country's *first inhabitants* are to be recognised, so must its *first nation.*

10

Fighting a war already won

Dallas Scott

Although Australians are a mix of cultures and heritages, the overwhelming and enduring spirit is to display a 'Fair Go'. Australians despise being called intolerant, or racist, and see themselves as more enlightened than most developing neighbours. They believe in fighting prejudice and righting wrongs, wherever they exist. It would seem that the current campaign for constitutional recognition is in keeping with that spirit. The former Labor Government spent millions of dollars in an 'education campaign', informing the public as to the benefits of voting 'Yes' to constitutional recognition for Aboriginal people.

It is inherently wrong that there is no mention in the Constitution of Aboriginal people as occupiers prior to British invasion of this land. If the Constitution is the equivalent of a birth certificate for the country, then it should list the facts. Unfortunately, unlike correcting a birth certificate for a child, correcting the Constitution is far more difficult than pointing out the omission to a registry official. A vote of all Australians is required to change the Constitution.

Sounds reasonably easy. This apparent wrong in our history can be put right. The reality is far more sobering. When it comes to referendums, there is a prevailing attitude of 'don't know, vote No'. Currently, more than 60 per cent of Australians are unaware of what constitutional recognition means. Add to this the fact that there is no

definitive proposition; the likely result will be an embarrassing failure.
It is an enormous gamble; at best a pleasant distraction.

The 1999 preamble

In the current debate, there are different approaches. The most radical
and least likely proposals to succeed are those that suggest new racial
discrimination measures be added to the Constitution, in addition to
any symbolic mention of Aboriginal people. The other, competing
school of thought, is that the greatest prospect of success is a limited
insertion of words that simply refer to Aboriginal occupation of
Australia prior to 1788. This latter is not a new proposal, but an idea
that has been tried before, and failed dismally.

On 6 October 1999, Australians were asked to make two tough
decisions. First, to become a Republic, second, to add a Preamble to
the Constitution. The proposed Preamble was carefully crafted and
included Aboriginal recognition. In addition to recognising Australia
as a land now made up of people from all backgrounds and a diverse
range of heritages, it included the following:

> ... honouring Aborigines and Torres Strait Islanders, the
> nation's first people, for their deep kinship with their lands
> and for their ancient and continuing cultures which enrich
> the life of our country.

The result was that a dismal 39 per cent of people voted yes for the
Preamble. The republic fared only slightly better, gaining the support
of 45 per cent of the voters. The result was not unexpected, in fact,
the last successful referendum occurred in 1977. In a nation where
there have been 44 referendums, only 8 of these have been successful.
Constitutional change is a risky, low-success option full of hazards
and little prospect of success.

In the current climate, the push for recognition serves only to illustrate the fact that, in Australia, there is a 'multi speed' Aboriginal society. At one end, a highly educated, mostly urban collective of voices with titles such as 'professor' or 'doctor', demanding far-reaching changes for 'their' people. The hypocrisy, apparently not evident to them, is that the very paternalism of the past they decry, they now wish to foist upon the least fortunate, least educated and most isolated.

The insulting part of the equation is that tens of millions of dollars in taxpayers' money is being gambled on this venture. The money is not proof that the idea has the support of Australians at large, but rather, 'the squeaky wheel gets the oil'. Those with the ear of the media and the disposable funds that allow them to set up websites for their causes, lobby government and pay for glossy advertisements, will inevitably be heard, funded or appeased. It is rather a stark illustration of the lack of democracy, or free speech, when it comes to 'First People'. Those who talk the loudest, and have the most power are those who overwhelmingly steer the issues – not the people at large. Sadly, this is the enduring legacy of Aboriginal affairs in Australia. Those given titles such as 'elder', 'spokesperson', 'tribal leader' (or some other colourful variations) are those not elected by the people they claim to represent, but overwhelmingly, are self-appointed to such a role. In a society where citizens have been sent to die for the chance to bring democracy to another country, some turn a blind eye to the undemocratic state of native organisations.

Those with no mandate to make decisions that affect people for whom they have no legitimacy to speak are most seen and heard. Such leaders embrace the notion of 'culture', but shy away from speaking about the practices that still exist and should not. Dysfunctional traditions such as 'humbugging' have largely been allowed, not only to continue, but also proliferate. Whilst not an issue that faces urban Aborigines in great numbers, those in communities who follow traditional practices like these with an almost religious fervour, are the ones who suffer the brunt of the fallout from this cultural practice. A hunter-gatherer tradition that no member of the tribe would go without has evolved in modern times to become a scourge upon the resources of the most needy.

It should not be this way. Instead of promises of false justice and selfish distractions like constitutional recognition real issues need to be addressed. Focusing energy and resources on a referendum, when efforts are required elsewhere to make real and lasting change, is a risky bet: change that is not dependant on mustering votes, bought, promised or begged, but on working on the most important issues. Those without a voice trust the rest who have one to speak up for them. They are not the ones lecturing on recognition from a function centre, but the people who are often functionally illiterate and unemployed, thousands of kilometres away from where people are listening and deciding what is important for them. I believe that these people, overwhelmingly, call for better housing, protection from violence and corruption, healthcare, jobs, education and the dignity that cannot be legislated into being.

The voiceless do not need another empty gesture. They have already had plenty. They have been assured time again of programs that will fix their ills. In reality, it was never going to be that simple. But they believed, and Australians spent billions over the decades reassuring them, that the answers were at hand. The infamous Mabo case did not magically return Aborigines happily to their homelands. When it was acknowledged that an unacceptably large number of Aboriginal people were leaving custody in a coffin, Australia got a Royal Commission into Aboriginal Deaths in Custody. But black men still die in jail today. Former Prime Minister Kevin Rudd took to a Canberra podium to declare that he was 'sorry'; an act long called for, but in the period that has elapsed it proved to be no more than a symbolic gesture. *Generation One, Close the Gap* and a multitude of other well-funded, well-branded and supported initiatives, so far, have not proved their worth where it counts - results. Aboriginal Australians are a people promised much, but delivered little.

Will constitutional recognition be any different?

Constitutional recognition is an exercise in futility. Unlike the resounding result achieved in 1967 that allowed native Australians to be counted in the Census, and to have laws made on their behalf, there is no urgency or importance attached to the present undertaking. At best, it appears to be mere semantics, at worst a terrible waste of energy, resources and misdirection from solving the real issues plaguing the most disadvantaged 'First People'. Programs have failed to solve issues that are both destroying lives and, more unforgivably, taking them, in the most disadvantaged Aboriginal communities and families across Australia.

If a referendum takes place, the votes are counted and, as expected, the proposed changes fail to pass, the outcomes for two groups will be a stark contrast. Those who led the charge will find other work, consoling themselves loudly to news outlets that it was not a surprise that things failed, considering what a horribly racist and ignorant bunch of people are Australians. Those who were promised big things would happen in their lives, if all went well, will feel resentment. The same resentment will slowly creep in, over weeks and months and years, as occurred after 'sorry'. 'Sorry', as the strange realisation hits that life would not drastically change, despite the many promises.

Resentment will not be directed at the better educated, city cousins who are largely responsible for making false promises, and to whom their anger should be directed. Instead, it will be directed to rank and file Australians. The 'smarter' Aborigines told them so. Australians have happily swallowed the lie that Aborigines are one big, multi-coloured, family who stick together. At least, that is, in front of the OTAs (Other Than Aborigines). Step beyond the crafted image and you will find family disputes that stretch back generations, conflict between and within 'tribes', and debate that exists on issues where it is claimed there is racial unity.

Pushing aside the promises made thus far about what constitutional recognition will and will not give Aboriginal people, and relying on the fact alone, Aboriginal Australians must look at themselves honestly and ask, what do I have to gain from constitutional recognition?

Stop fighting a war already won

As a native Australian, it would be nice to have a constitution that makes mention of our occupation of this great country for tens of thousands of years. The reality, however, is that it will not change nor improve my life. It will not give my people back their land, land already fought for and won, but for the last decade, in some areas, under government control. It will not improve life expectancy or literacy. It will not make a dent in rates of alcohol abuse, domestic violence or improve health services for the most needy. It will not erase racism, assure justice or provide protection from corruption. It will not provide the catalyst to change incarceration rates, or overrepresentation in prison populations. These are legacies that I am ashamed to be leaving to my children, and others of their generation, as a native of this country - not our omission in the Constitution.

These are the children who are now taught about Aboriginal occupation prior to the arrival of Captain Cook as standard in our national curriculum.

Far from being invisible, or denied our rightful place, we have reached a place where these are embraced, accepted and commonplace. We should stop fighting a war already won, and focus energies on the wars yet to be won. Of those, there is no shortage.

International follies

11

Constitutionalising Canadian Aboriginal rights

Tom Flanagan

I f Australians want to put Aborigines and Torres Strait Islanders into the Constitution, they will be wise to look at the experience of Canada, which took a similar step for its aboriginal peoples in 1982. It is sobering to look at the consequences of that action in Canada.

With one interruption of less than a year, Pierre Elliott Trudeau was Prime Minister of Canada from 1968 to 1984. The main reason he entered politics was to reformulate relations between English and French citizens and to turn Canada into a truly bilingual country. The main instrument of that transformation was supposed to be a constitutional charter of rights. The original focus was on language rights, but in his long quest to build political support for his charter, Trudeau offered concessions to many interest groups concerned with other issues. As a result, the 1982 constitutional amendment package containing the Canadian *Charter of Rights and Freedoms* also contained these provisions on aboriginal rights:

> 25. The guarantee in this Charter of certain rights and freedoms shall not be construed so as to abrogate or derogate from any aboriginal, treaty or other rights or freedoms that pertain to the aboriginal peoples of Canada including:
>
> (a) any rights or freedoms that have been recognized by the Royal Proclamation of October 7, 1763, and

(b) any rights or freedoms that now exist by way of land claims agreements or may be so acquired.

35. (1) The existing aboriginal and treaty rights of the aboriginal peoples of Canada are hereby recognized and affirmed.

(2) In this Act, 'aboriginal peoples of Canada' includes the Indian, Inuit and Métis peoples of Canada.

(3) For greater certainty, in subsection (1) 'treaty rights' includes rights that now exist by way of land claims agreements or may be so acquired.

(4) Notwithstanding any other provision of this Act, the aboriginal and treaty rights referred to in subsection (1) are guaranteed equally to male and female persons.

The remarkable thing about these clauses is how open-ended they were. The term 'aboriginal peoples of Canada' was enumerated as 'the Indian, Inuit, and Métis peoples of Canada,' but these categories were left undefined, even though all had been the subject of disputes for decades. Nor were the rights themselves spelled out, except to say that 'treaty rights' would include 'land claims agreements', which is a term often used for contemporary treaties. One provincial premier, concerned about the vagueness, was able to get the word 'existing' inserted before 'aboriginal and treaty rights' in section 35 (1), on the basis of the theory – widely accepted at the time – that the signing of treaties had already extinguished aboriginal rights based on prior occupancy, but the word 'existing' has had little impact upon subsequent jurisprudence.

Consequently, the net effect of these open-ended constitutional amendments was to transfer to the judiciary decision-making power over many aspects of aboriginal affairs. In the common-law tradition, the courts are the interpreters of the Constitution. If the language is vague, judges have to fill in the gaps. And it is not just judges who are empowered. Common-law courts choose between legal theories offered to them by counsel who argue on behalf of the litigants. So the aboriginal bar frames the issues, assisted by clerks who work for them, informed by law-school professors, whose stock in trade is the invention of novel legal theories, and consultants in history and anthropology who offer supporting social-science evidence.

All of this was a net transfer of power from the parliamentary to the judicial arena. Of course, there had been aboriginal litigation before 1982, but in most cases judges were interpreting common-law aboriginal rights, or statutes and treaties, but not the Constitution. If Parliament did not like the court's interpretation, it could pass new legislation to override it or specify nuances. Now, however, court decisions became final, because the Charter had made all aboriginal and treaty rights constitutional. From that point on, judicial interpretations of these rights could not be overridden by ordinary legislation, but only by constitutional amendment; and in practice, it has become almost impossible to amend the Canadian Constitution, so that decisions of the Supreme Court of Canada regarding aboriginal and treaty rights are effectively final.

Duty to consult

As critics of judicial activism predicted would happen, judges, lawyers, and law schools have picked up the constitutional football and run with it. In a little more than 30 years since the adoption of the Charter, aboriginal affairs have been fundamentally transformed by court decisions. Let me describe the impact of one line of jurisprudence – the 'duty to consult', as rooted in the 'honour of the Crown'.

The honour of the Crown is an old concept in Canadian law. As originally understood, it meant that the courts would not tolerate cheating, deception, or sharp practice by Canadian officials when dealing with aboriginal people. Canada would have to live up to its agreements, and those agreements would have to be honestly, clearly, and fully explained. More recently, however, the honour of the Crown has metastasized into the ability of the courts to strike down decades-old agreements and administrative practices because they do not meet the latest (ever-evolving) standards of human rights activists. Consider these words of the Chief Justice of Canada in the crucial *Haida Nation* case (2004):

- The government's duty to consult with Aboriginal peoples and accommodate their interests is grounded in the honour of the Crown. The honour of the Crown is always at stake in its dealings with Aboriginal peoples. It is not a mere incantation, but rather a core precept that finds its application in concrete practices.

- The historical roots of the principle of the honour of the Crown suggest that it must be understood generously in order to reflect the underlying realities from which it stems. In all its dealings with Aboriginal peoples, from the assertion of sovereignty to the resolution of claims and the implementation of treaties, the Crown must act honourably.

- The honour of the Crown gives rise to different duties in different circumstances. Where the Crown has assumed discretionary control over specific Aboriginal interests, the honour of the Crown gives rise to a Fiduciary duty ... .

- The honour of the Crown also infuses the processes of treaty making and treaty interpretation. In making and applying treaties, the Crown must act with honour and integrity, avoiding even the appearance of sharp Dealing ... .

The sharp end of the stick in this decision was 'the duty to consult and, where indicated, accommodate Aboriginal interests,' presented as a logical consequence of the honour of the Crown. To understand the duty to consult, one has to know a bit about the circumstances of the case. The Haida Nation, like most First Nations in the province of British Columbia, has never signed a treaty ceding its aboriginal title to the Crown. Thus, in addition to its land reserves assigned by the provincial government, the Haida Nation still has unextinguished aboriginal title to the larger 'traditional territory' on which it lived prior to settling on land reserves. The provincial government wanted to issue a license for a tree farm on part of this traditional territory, but the Haida claimed they had not been sufficiently consulted about the impact of the license upon their interests.

The Canadian courts, culminating in the Supreme Court of Canada, affirmed British Columbia's duty to consult with the Haida about the proposed tree farm, though the courts also concluded that, in this particular case, the consultation had been adequate. Someday, they will presumably sign a treaty that will give them outright ownership of part of this traditional territory, so they have an interest in seeing that the value of the land is not degraded before a treaty is concluded.

Since 2004, subsequent judicial decisions have extended the duty to consult to other provinces, and to other situations – not only unceded lands, but 'traditional territories' surrounding reserves created as a result of treaties signed a century or more ago. But while extending the doctrine's applicability, the courts have left many aspects unclarified. They have said that consultation is the duty of government but that government may delegate the consultation, at least to some degree, to corporations or other entities. How much delegation is allowed is a question of judgment that the courts have never answered with clarity. Similarly, the courts have said that the greater the impact of a

project on First Nations, the greater the level of consultation required
– but without putting any metrics on these concepts. With this lack of
bright lines, the doctrine of the duty to consult has become an open
invitation to second-guessing in the courts. Native litigants have lost
many of these cases, but the very possibility of seeking judicial review,
and the multiple levels of appeal allowed in Canadian law introduces
an important element of expense and uncertainty into many resource
development projects.

The time and expense are usually bearable for geographically
delimited projects, such as oil and gas drilling, or a single mine, where
one can deal with a relatively small number of First Nations. Things
become much more difficult, however, in the case of a major oil or gas
pipeline, which would cross the 'traditional territories' of dozens of
First Nations. A useful pipeline has to transit all of these territories; it
only takes one 'holdout' First Nation to cause the whole pipeline to
fail. When many actors are involved in negotiating a bargain, everyone
is tempted to hang back, waiting to see what others get, then raise the
ante with new demands. This 'n-person Prisoner's Dilemma' can drive
costs so high that a project becomes uneconomic.

Northern Gateway pipeline

The most important case in contemporary Canada is the proposed
Northern Gateway pipeline, which would move oil from Alberta's
oil sands to a new port on the coast of British Columbia for export
to Asian markets. Canada badly needs a pipeline of this type. At
the present time, almost all Canadian oil exports go to the United
States, but that country's need is decreasing because of domestic
tight (fracking) oil discoveries. In addition, there is not enough
pipeline capacity to serve present exports to the United States, so that
Canadian heavy oil is selling at a discount, even though refineries on

the Gulf Coast would love to have it to replace decreasing supplies of Venezuelan heavy oil.

Fifteen or twenty years ago, Northern Gateway could probably have been built without too much opposition, but the new doctrine of duty to consult has given enormous leverage to the dozens of First Nations in northern Alberta and British Columbia. The pipeline would not cross their reserves, but they all have 'traditional territories' that are Crown land from a provincial point of view, but are subject to future claims in virtue of aboriginal title. The Northern Gateway proposal has been approved by the National Energy Board after years of hearings and is expected to receive Cabinet approval within a few months, but that does not mean it will be built. Dozens of First Nations, who have been stirred up and subsidised by American environmental non-government organisations, can be expected to oppose it in court on grounds of insufficient consultation. Even if the proponents of Northern Gateway win every case, the total of all cases could delay the project so long that it becomes uneconomic. That is more or less what happened to the Mackenzie Valley gas pipeline, first proposed in the 1970s and still not built 40 years later, even though all relevant governmental authorities approved it. Native opposition dragged on for so long that the project became uneconomic after shale gas discoveries. Had it been built when first proposed, it would have transformed much of Canada's north and brought wealth to industry and First Nations alike.

The Northern Gateway story continues. Maybe a deal can be struck that will resolve everyone's concerns, allowing the pipeline to be built and oil to be exported to Asia. But if I were an Australian pondering whether to recognise Aboriginal rights in the Constitution, I would be looking long and hard at the Canadian experience, asking if I wanted to hand over so much power to judges, lawyers, and Aboriginal litigants. Australia, like Canada, is an export-oriented natural-resource powerhouse, whose prosperity depends on moving products to external markets. Neither country can afford to burden itself with judge-made legal doctrines that take no account of economic realities.

12

Neo-tribal elites want more from New Zealanders

David Round

In New Zealand, as in Australia, a small radical remnant of a pre-European 'indigenous' race is attempting to hijack the Constitution by the insertion of clauses guaranteeing racial preference.

Maori have a far feebler claim than the aboriginal inhabitants of Australia, resident for an inconceivable age, to be considered 'indigenous'. They reached New Zealand no earlier than about 1200 AD, and possibly a little later. They may have had visitors – Chinese, Tamil, Spanish and Portuguese – well before Abel Tasman sailed by in 1642. Only five hundred and fifty years separate the arrival of Maori from Captain Cook's landing in 1769. That event was almost two and a half centuries ago. The European history of New Zealand, then, is already at least almost half the length of time when Maori may have had the islands to themselves.

Nor is there any longer any distinct and separate Maori race. By intermarriage and friendship Maori and Briton have largely become one people. A more inclusive definition has replaced the older statutory one of Maori as requiring a moiety of Maori ancestry. A Maori is merely 'a person of the Maori race of New Zealand; and includes any descendant of such a person'. There would be far fewer Maori, for example, were the test that found in the *Alaska Settlement Act 1971* (US), which requires 'one-fourth degree or more Alaskan Indian, Eskimo or Aleut blood', or, in the absence of proof of such blood quantum, a very clearly defined ancestral cultural and community identification. Most New Zealanders of Maori ancestry are indistinguishable, in appearance and actual living culture, from anyone else.

Identification as 'Maori' is fluid and changeable, and for most of those who do so identify, ancient tribal structures and affiliations have little if any serious practical relevance, at least beyond any possible financial benefit. Professor Elizabeth Rata argues that modern Maori 'tribes' are better seen as 'capitalist neo-tribal elites' rather than as living communities sharing a common descent.

Constitutional void

New Zealand has no identifiable written Constitution. The original Imperial statute, the *New Zealand Constitution Act 1852*, is no more; the very brief *Constitution Act 1986* is little more than a collection of headings; the *Electoral Act 1993* runs to the opposite extreme, with 520 sections of the most prosaic detail, and the *Bill of Rights Act 1990* has no independent over-riding force. New Zealand has no federal system; its one chamber of parliament, the House of Representatives, now elected by proportional representation, enjoys supreme power. The New Zealand Constitution is, *mutatis mutandis*, as was said of the 19th century British Constitution, 'a majority of one in the House of Commons'.

Alas, the chattering classes are determined to have New Zealand conform to the general Western trend away from democracy and towards a regime of *mores* awaiting discovery and amplification in a written constitution by a well-entrenched ruling caste of judicial activists and politically-correct academics and bureaucrats. Such is the contempt for the will of the people among the intelligentsia that the current Chief Justice can announce her judicial right to strike down the Acts of our supreme lawmaker if they clash with her own understanding of 'Treaty principles' or international law. There can be little doubt that were a written constitution to refer in any way to 'Treaty principles' – the New Zealand equivalent of mention of Australian aborigines as original indigenous inhabitants – the judiciary would seize upon any such reference as an opportunity for asserting their own supremacy over elected assemblies. Chris Trotter has observed that '[t]he extraordinary fact of the past forty years of our history is the manner in which this bold rejection of Captain Hobson's famous declaration at Waitangi – *he iwi tahi tatou* – now we are one people – has become the official policy of the New Zealand state'.

Constitutionalising the Treaty of Waitangi

Since British sovereignty was established in New Zealand in 1840, all Maori have enjoyed, in the words of the Treaty of Waitangi's third article, 'the rights and privileges of British subjects'. Nor was New Zealand ever thought to be *terra nullius*; the courts have always recognised the principle of aboriginal title. The Treaty's second article specifically recognises the right of the native inhabitants to their 'lands, forests and fisheries'.

The Treaty itself has no independent legal standing, either in international law or as part of New Zealand's domestic law. Despite its name, the 'Treaty' was merely a memorandum of understanding, preliminary to the later acquisition of sovereignty. Treaty activists seldom deny this point, still constantly acknowledged judicially, but the Treaty's lack of legal status is consistently disregarded as it is emphasised to be the political basis, if not the 'founding document', of the New Zealand state.

The new radical Maori claim for special constitutional recognition has, therefore, a legalistic quality to it. Rather than base a claim to special treatment on a highly arguable status as indigenous, or a more blatant 'first come first served' principle, the argument used is one likelier to appeal to a law-respecting and fair-minded people. It is that the 'principles' of the Treaty, referred to occasionally by Parliament since 1975, but never given any statutory definition, should now be 'enshrined' in law. This is the clear desire of the Maori Party, part of the current National Party-led government coalition, when it succeeded in having an official Constitutional Advisory Panel established in 2010.

The success of such an approach, however, depends on a misrepresentation of what Treaty principles are. The 'principles' were first mentioned only when the Waitangi Tribunal was established in 1975 to investigate laws and government policies and actions allegedly established or done in breach of these undefined principles. Parliaments did not then, or at any time thereafter, define them. The Tribunal itself defined them. (The Tribunal must always have a majority of Maori members, and has regularly displayed blatant bias and flagrant disregard of elementary evidential principles. Some of its reports have excited widespread derision.) The Tribunal, which is mercifully not a court, could then make 'recommendations' on claims laid before it.

In 1985, the government gave the Tribunal a retrospective jurisdiction to 1840, and so opened the floodgates to an enormous number of historical claims, including those that had *already* been the subject of 'full and final settlements'. At the same time, a number of other statutes began to mention Treaty 'principles', and in 1987, the Court of Appeal made the first of many judicial interpretations and interventions on behalf of 'Treaty principles'. The Court of

Appeal's principles were vague and worthy platitudes involving mutual obligation and good faith. Their emphasis on honourable behaviour and good faith between the parties might also contain the unfortunate implication that New Zealanders, not of Maori descent, were not entitled to the same degree of fair dealing from the Crown.

But it was the Court's references to 'partners' and 'partnership' which have perhaps had the most unfortunate consequences. The Court used the word 'partners' very loosely, and interchangeably with the word 'parties'. But now the 'Treaty partnership' is spoken of as a matter of course. Without any need for explanation, Treatyists now universally accept it as an obvious and indisputable fact. It is, in fact, the very opposite of what the Treaty says, that Maori are to be equal with Briton under the Queen's law, and therefore entitled, as are all subjects, to their property.

The Treaty's *actual terms* – the equality of all citizens under the law – are an excellent thing and are reflected in New Zealand law. They are no recipe for special rights. They are no more than the basic outlines of a legal system respecting racial equality, property rights and the rule of law. But the terms are now forgotten. The Treaty has passed into myth; like Magna Carta, it has become a hazy blank slate onto which any and all desires may be projected. The Treaty's actual words contain no partnership. The Treaty was, moreover, an agreement whereby Maori voluntarily extinguished whatever sovereignty they may have enjoyed in return for the blessings of the *pax Britannica*.

If Maori are the Queen's partners, then they cannot be her subjects as are the rest of New Zealand. Whether the 15 per cent or so of the population identifying themselves as 'Maori' are the equal partner of the 'Crown' or of the non-Maori population, in either case it would follow that that equal partner is entitled to an equal share in representation, law-making and government. A democracy of equal citizens goes out the window and in the door come racial quotas and 'co-management'.

Consequences of recognition

The consequences of constitutional recognition of Treaty principles would resonate through every aspect of New Zealand life. Although the last twenty years have seen exhaustive negotiations and the 'full and final settlement' of 'historical' Treaty claims, many Maori are openly saying that no settlement of 'historical' grievances can ever be final. A 2006 amendment to the Waitangi Tribunal's jurisdiction prevents the lodging of further claims referring to events before 1992, but since then the Tribunal has entertained a claim to – and made dubious recommendations on – the ownership of water, a matter that was finally settled by statute in 1967. Given the enthusiasm for Treaty principles among some of the higher judiciary, there can be little doubt but that any constitutional recognition of principles would guarantee the continuation of 'historical' Treaty claims, as well as further claims of present-day injustice, forever. Those identifying as Maori will be cast as perpetual victims and perpetual parasites, and no-one will benefit except that neo-tribal elite.

But that would be only the beginning. Already Maori claim special rights over the public conservation estate (about one third of New Zealand's land area), claim the 'taonga' promised them under the Treaty, which now allegedly includes such previously unthought-of abstractions as their own language and 'culture', and such things as radio waves and underground oil and gas. Already, local authorities are recording sacred sites of various sorts over private property – often without any necessity for physical evidence – and thereafter landowners may not interfere with those sacred values without the consent of local Maori. Special Maori representation, quite unrelated to population, is demanded and sometimes granted on local bodies. The Parliamentary Maori seats are vigorously defended, even though their abolition was recommended by the 1986 Report of the Royal Commission on the Electoral System, which considered them unnecessary after proportional representation was established.

The New Zealand Maori Council has declared that elderly Maori people are a 'taonga' who, therefore, are entitled to racial preference in the distribution of limited health care. Some academic institutions have racial quotas of various sorts, and compulsory Maori cultural indoctrination is a feature of considerable parts of tertiary education. It also features largely at primary and secondary levels. The explanation now offered, even by the United Nations, for the high proportion of the prison population of Maori descent – somewhere around half – is bias in the administration of justice, rather than the simple sad fact that a higher proportion of those of Maori descent commit serious and violent crimes.

Prominent and influential forces are arguing for the replacement of a democracy of equal citizens with a Balkanised 'Aotearoa' where ones primary identification will be with ones 'tribe' – 'Ngati Maori', 'Ngati Pakeha', 'Ngati Pasifika', 'Ngati Asia'. Radical Treaty ideology permeates the ranks of academia and the judiciary. The ruling class completely fails to recognise the dangers of increasing racial division, and has no solution to increasing popular resentment other than to despise and ignore it, and attempt its official suppression.

While the settlement of historical grievances was in full swing, New Zealanders were assured that, following settlement, the past could be put behind them. That was a colossal lie. The Constitutional Advisory Panel, for example, was established in 2010 as part of the

National Party's coalition deal with the Maori Party because the Maori Party believed there was a 'need', as well as a requirement in the Treaty itself, to put the Treaty and its alleged 'guarantees' into a constitution in order to 'protect' Maori.

Maori put forward a highly unlikely political scenario - that after achieving some separate, or even independent status, both they and the greater population they have striven so hard to reject, would then be willing and able to co-operate for the greater good. What prevents them from doing that now? It is not unreasonable to suspect that, after achieving separateness, they would still expect financial support from their alienated fellow citizens. Metiria Turei, currently the co-leader of the Green Party and formerly its spokesperson on Maori Affairs, saw no absurdity in claiming in your author's hearing in 2005 that 'Maori want two things – they want independence, and they want more funding'.

To suggest that one particular racial group needs special constitutional recognition in order to protect it from the depredations of its fellow-citizens is not a very happy or hopeful analysis of the national situation. New Zealand's Treaty agitation is remarkable in that it seeks the very opposite of what was sought by South Africa's black freedom movement and the civil rights movement in the United States. Those movements sought genuine equality, as opposed to a 'separate but equal' status, which was of course, not equal at all.

13

Great constitution, shame about the nation

Kerryn Pholi and Gary Johns

Many national constitutions recognise indigenous inhabitants. How they do so, and what benefits the recognition carries depends more on the history and circumstances of the inclusion, and the surrounding politics, than on the words. The inclusion is no guarantee of the success of indigenous people. Indeed, some of the finest words belie some of the most shocking treatments: the 'bill of rights' US and the 'dictatorial' Zimbabwe both recognise their indigenous people. An 'illiberal' Chile and 'liberal' Australia do not. This chapter discusses the different aims of recognition and the nations that use the device.

Recognition of exclusive rights for 'First Australians'

If the purpose of the campaign for constitutional change is to establish a separate set of rights for Aboriginal people simply because they are 'First Australians', at the very least, the precise nature of these rights should be clearly expressed. The Constitution of Sweden acknowledges 'the right of the Sami population to practise reindeer husbandry', for example, while the Constitution of South Africa recognises the role of 'traditional leadership as an institution at local level on matters affecting local communities'. Such an approach could, for example, recognise the rights of Aboriginal Australians to enjoy a monopoly over distinctly recognisable Aboriginal cultural practices, or perhaps to maintain certain traditional systems of local governance. The Constitution would, in this event, need to define precisely the acceptable distinct and exclusive cultural practices of Aboriginal Australians.

Alternatively, the Constitution could recognise the specialness of Aboriginal Australians in the manner of Fiji's Preamble to its Constitution. The Preamble recognises 'the unique culture, customs, traditions and languages' of the iTaukei and Rotuman indigenous peoples, along with the descendants of the indentured labourers from British India and the Pacific Islands, and the descendants of the settlers and immigrants to Fiji. In short, Fiji's preamble effectively acknowledges that everybody in Fiji belongs to some ethnic or cultural group that has a unique culture, customs, traditions and languages. The recognition has not solved Fiji's interminable inter-ethnic jealousies, these being the basis of the Commodore Frank Bainimarama coup of 2006 and earlier coups.

Following Fiji's even-handed example, Australia could maintain its egalitarian ethos by acknowledging the uniqueness and specialness of Aboriginal Australians, while also acknowledging that every other Australian is also unique and special. Of course, Australia could opt for a simpler and cheaper means of achieving the same result, by simply refraining from acknowledging anybody in Australia as being more or less special than anybody else.

Recognition of unique Aboriginal culture and knowledge

If the purpose of constitutional recognition is to ensure that Australian governments take measures to preserve traditional Aboriginal cultural practices and languages for future Aboriginal people to enjoy, the Constitution of Zimbabwe may offer a useful model:

The state must take measures to preserve, protect and promote indigenous knowledge systems, including knowledge of the medicinal and other properties of animal and plant life possessed by local communities and people.

The Zimbabwean approach does not recognise that certain groups of citizens possess a distinct set of traditional or cultural rights, or that access to opportunities and exemptions should be afforded to certain citizens over others. Rather, the Constitution of Zimbabwe recognises that traditional knowledge exists and that the state has a role to play in its preservation, protection and promotion. Recognition does not necessarily oblige the Zimbabwean state to support or promote the lifestyles of certain individuals or groups on the basis of their indigenous heritage.

The context for recognition in Zimbabwe was the election in 1980 of Prime Minister Robert Mugabe. Later President, Mugabe was knighted in 1994 by Queen Elizabeth II, for 'significant contributions' to relations between Britain and Zimbabwe. The Queen revoked the knighthood in 2008 because of 'The abuse of human rights and abject disregard for the democratic process in Zimbabwe over which President Mugabe has presided.'

Recognition as a gesture of respect and reconciliation

If the intention of constitutional recognition of Aboriginal cultural rights is a symbolic gesture toward reconciliation, perhaps this sensible, pragmatic statement in the Constitution of Indonesia could serve as a guide:

The cultural identities and rights of traditional communities shall be respected in accordance with the development of times and civilisations.

Such a statement elegantly acknowledges that respect for traditional culture cannot be both genuine and unconditional at the same time. It offers respect for traditional cultures without the banality of cultural relativism, and acknowledges that no culture, whether modern or traditional, should expect to remain unchanged.

National constitutions that recognise the existence of indigenous or traditional cultural rights tend to do so within the context of a 'bill of rights' for all citizens. This allows the Constitution to set clear guidelines around the co-existence of 'cultural' rights within broader citizenship rights. Nations such as Singapore, South Africa, Kenya and many others recognise that their indigenous citizens are differentiated. Indigenous citizens can be children, women, elderly, disabled, or simply different in ways that make them particularly vulnerable to isolation, neglect, exploitation and predation within a 'traditional' culture.

The Constitution of Singapore, for example, recognises Malays as the indigenous people of Singapore, and acknowledges the state's role in promoting the social and cultural interests of Malay people – yet the Singaporean Constitution also contains a detailed discussion of the overarching rights and liberties of all citizens. The Constitution of South Africa acknowledges the state's role in supporting traditional cultures and preserving indigenous languages, yet it also states that:

> Everyone has the right to use the language and to participate in the cultural life of their choice, but no one exercising these rights may do so in a manner inconsistent with any provision of the Bill of Rights.

Similarly, the Mexican Constitution allows for indigenous 'legal systems to regulate and solve their internal conflicts, subjected to the general principles of this Constitution, respecting the fundamental rights, the human rights and, above all, the dignity and safety of women.'

The Constitution of Kenya also makes clear that any cultural practices are subservient to the rights of children to education and care, and subservient to the rights of other vulnerable people – such as the elderly – to exercise freely the full range of their rights as Kenyan citizens. The Kenyan Constitution also includes the clause, 'A person shall not compel another person to perform, observe or undergo any cultural practice or rite.' Should the recognition of Aboriginal cultural rights become a feature of the Australian Constitution, it may be wise to include such a clause, to ensure that neglect of, or violence upon, vulnerable members of Aboriginal communities is not excused as a 'cultural practice or rite'.

Individual rights must always take precedence over the expression of traditional, cultural rights. For example, the right of every Aboriginal woman to live free from violence must take precedence over any Aboriginal man's cultural right to hit his wife on the head with a stick. In order to protect the rights of vulnerable Aboriginal citizens, the Constitution would have to set out the rights of citizens in general - and perhaps in detail the rights of particular groups of citizens such as women, children, the elderly and the disabled.

The Rwandan Constitution contains a bill of rights, but it also includes a clause that limits the enjoyment of traditional practices and the expression of cultural rights.

> The State has the duty to safeguard and to promote positive values based on cultural traditions and practices so long as they do not conflict with human rights, public order and good morals.

Australians would probably feel inclined to retain the 'human rights' in the clause above, and dispense with the old-fashioned 'public order' and embarrassingly quaint 'good morals'. Perhaps Australia could learn much from the experiences of nations such as Rwanda, which have learned hard lessons about the value of public order, a shared sense of basic morality, and the need for careful management of 'cultural diversity'.

Recognition to address Aboriginal disadvantage and 'close the gap'

The constitutions of some nations include measures to ensure the protection, promotion or advancement of certain groups, in the interests of fairness and/or social equality. It is made clear that special measures are required because these groups are presently disadvantaged. The Constitution of India, for example, refers to measures for the benefit of tribes and other groups considered 'weak and backward', while the Constitution of Tanzania acknowledges 'certain categories of people are regarded as weak or inferior' and, therefore, require special measures 'aimed at rectifying disabilities in the society'.

If the Australian Constitution is to contain references to special measures for the advancement of Aboriginal people in the interests of 'closing the gap', it should contain a justification for these measures. The Constitution may, therefore, need to acknowledge either that Aboriginal people are presently so 'backward' that they cannot function as ordinary citizens, or that broader Australian society is so inherently unjust that Aboriginal people require state intervention. It is very doubtful that Australia is so divided and troubled that it should consider adopting such a measure. Do Australians of Aboriginal descent wish to be defined in the Constitution as 'weak, backward and inferior' in perpetuity, or at all?

Aboriginal Australians and other supporters of constitutional change may be happy to accept the label of 'backwardness', if it secures access to special rights and resources for their 'advancement'. That such a measure creates an incentive to remain 'backward' forever would concern many Australians. India's Constitution contains sunset provisions on its special measures for the advancement of 'Scheduled Castes', 'Scheduled Tribes' and/or 'Other Backward Classes'. Similar sunset provisions on measures to 'close the gap' in Australia may offer some reassurance to voters. India's Constitution bristles with amendments referring to its ever-evolving 'Backward Classes', and with extensions upon extensions of the end-dates for special measures to resolve their persistent backwardness.

Land rights

A number of nations use their constitution to resolve the difficulties for indigenous people of access to land. The US Constitution, for example, contains some very quaint language, wherein Section 2 on the apportionment of numbers of voters for state representation, excludes Indians 'not taxed'. The present taxation of American Indians means that they are counted for purposes of apportionment.

Section 8 of the US Constitution regulates 'Commerce with Foreign Nations, and among the several States, and with the Indian Tribes', reflecting the historical fact that the young American state drew up treaties with Indian tribes as a means of settling disputes between settlers and Indians and settling reserves of land. The 'Indian commerce clause' has become the main source of power for congressional legislation dealing with those now known as Native Americans.

The Constitution of Argentina in Section 25 expresses the

racist sentiment that the Federal government shall 'foster European immigration'. Shades of Australia's white Australia policy, long ago abandoned, and never placed in the Constitution. Nevertheless, and in spite of those Argentinian sentiments, section 75 recognises

> the community possession and ownership of the lands they [Indians] traditionally occupy; and to regulate the granting of other lands adequate and sufficient for human development; none of them shall be sold, transmitted or subject to liens or attachments.

The union [nation], nevertheless, owns those lands traditionally occupied by Indians.

The Constitution of Brazil contains an entire chapter on Indians. Among other aspects of recognition, Article 231 states that 'Indians shall have their ... original rights to the lands they traditionally occupy, it being incumbent upon the Union to demarcate them, protect and ensure respect for all of their property.' The Constitution guarantees 'the lands traditionally occupied by Indians are intended for their permanent possession and they shall have the exclusive usufruct of the riches of the soil, the rivers and the lakes existing therein.' With respect to energy and mineral resources, these 'may only be exploited, ... with the authorisation of the National Congress, after hearing the communities involved.'

Conclusion

The most sensible approach to the demand for constitutional recognition of Aboriginal people is to either not accede to the demand, or express simple acknowledgement of historical fact in a preamble. If substantive constitutional changes to recognise Aboriginal Australians as a separate and distinct group in possession of specific entitlements and cultural rights were pursued, the experiences of nations whose constitutions already divide their citizenry by race, ethnicity or culture are instructive. If any of those nations' paths are the intended one for Australia, their reasoning, successes and failures should be carefully examined.

Contributors

Wesley Aird works on solving problems so that indigenous Australians can become genuine participants in the real economy. His primary work is with resource sector companies in the management of native title and cultural heritage and also in the development of initiatives for indigenous employment, training and business. Wesley maintains a very strong commitment to his own community on the Gold Coast through both native title and cultural heritage.

James Allan is the Garrick Professor of Law at the University of Queensland. He has practised law in Canada and was at the Bar in London. He has taught in Hong Kong, New Zealand and Australia, with sabbaticals at Cornell, Osgoode Hall, San Diego and as the Bertha Wilson Visiting Professor of Human Rights in Nova Scotia. He writes regularly for *The Australian, Spectator Australia and Quadrant.* He is strongly opposed to bills of rights and over-powerful judges.

Ron Brunton is a Queensland anthropologist who has been writing about and consulting on native title and Aboriginal cultural heritage issues for over twenty years. He has taught anthropology in universities in Australia and Papua New Guinea and worked in the Commonwealth Public Service and private industry. He has also been a fortnightly columnist for *The Courier-Mail,* and a board member of the Australian Broadcasting Corporation. He is currently working on the centenary history of the Alexandra Headland Surf Life Saving Club.

Alistair Crooks is a geologist whose first encounter with remote area Aborigines was in the early seventies in the bush 100 kilometres south west of Tennant Creek. Intrigued and impressed, this encounter, and many subsequent encounters during his career working both with and for Aborigines, has resulted in a lifelong interest in traditional Aboriginal culture, and a real concern for Aboriginal people who can at times become victims of that culture.

Anthony Dillon identifies as a part-Aboriginal Australian. Anthony is a lecturer at the Australian Catholic University. He regularly comments on indigenous issues and is co-editor of *In Black and White: Australians All at the Crossroads*. His passion is promoting discussion on how best to help the most disadvantaged Aborigines to attain a standard of living most Australians take for granted. He believes that an excessive focus on culture, political correctness, and with blaming white Australia has placed too many Aborigines in an early grave. He wishes to thank Nigel Parbury for his assistance in his chapter.

Tom Flanagan is a Distinguished Fellow at the School of Public Policy, University of Calgary, and a Fellow of the Royal Society of Canada. He is the author of several books on Aboriginal affairs, including *First Nations? Second Thoughts* and *Beyond the Indian Act: Restoring Aboriginal Property Rights*. Tom serves on the Board of Directors of the Society for Academic Freedom and Scholarship.

Gary Johns is Adjunct Professor at QUT Business School and a columnist for *The Australian* newspaper. He served in the House of Representatives and in the Keating Governments. He was an Associate Commissioner of the Commonwealth Productivity Commission. Gary received the Centenary Medal and the Fulbright Professional Award in Australian-United States Alliance Studies, served at Georgetown University Washington DC. He was Senior Fellow Institute of Public Affairs, senior consultant ACIL Tasman, and Associate Professor at the Australian Catholic University.

† **Bryan Pape** was an International Commercial Arbitrator. He practised at the New South Wales and Victorian Bars in taxation

and constitutional law matters. In 2010, he gave the Third Sir Harry Gibbs Memorial Oration to the Samuel Griffith Society on 'Stopping Stimulus Spending'. He was a former senior lecturer in the School of Law in the University of New England and was a sometime member of both the Taxation Board of Review No.1 and the Australian Accounting Standards Board.

Kerryn Pholi is a former Aboriginal public servant, social worker and teacher, currently working within the justice system. She has worked in research and policy in a number of government agencies and non-government organisations, primarily in data collection and reporting on Aboriginal health and wellbeing. Her articles on identity politics and freedom of speech have appeared in *Quadrant*, *Spectator Australia* and *The Drum*.

David Round is a sixth-generation New Zealander who teaches environmental law, land law and legal history and philosophy at the University of Canterbury. He wrote *Truth or Treaty? Commonsense Questions about the Treaty of Waitangi*, and he is a contributor to *Twisting the Treaty, A Tribal Grab for Wealth and Power*. He stood for parliament for the National Party in 2005, and more recently was the chair of the Independent Constitutional Review Panel, established to counter the official Constitutional Advisory Panel.

Frank Salter heads the consultancy, Social Technologies P/L, which analyses management and policy. His academic background is urban anthropology and ethology, the biological study of social behaviour. Initially trained at Sydney and Griffith universities, he researched and taught at the Max Planck Institute for Human Ethology near Munich, Germany, a period that included teaching in Britain, the US, and Russia. His books include *Emotions in Command: Biology, Bureaucracy, and Cultural Evolution,* and *On Genetic Interests: Family, Ethnicity and Humanity in an Age of Mass Migration.*

Dallas Scott was born in 1973, the youngest of three children to Campbell Carter (Lake Tyers) and Christine Scott (Wallaga Lake). As a toddler, he was placed into care (along with his brother) and raised in Ferntree Gully, at the foothills of the Dandenong Ranges in Victoria; by a wonderful couple he calls Mum and Dad, Irene and Ray Christoffersen. Today, he is a husband, father of four children and a full-time carer, his most important jobs to date. Still living in Victoria, he writes in his spare time and with one goal – to have his say and speak for himself.

www.ingramcontent.com/pod-product-compliance
Lightning Source LLC
Chambersburg PA
CBHW020615270326
41927CB00005B/341